GOD IS NOT GOD'S NAME

A Journey Beyond Words

Stephen Edington

Order this book online at www.trafford.com
or email orders@trafford.com

Most Trafford titles are also available at major online book retailers.

Print information available on the last page.

ISBN: 978-1-4907-8966-8 (sc)
ISBN: 978-1-4907-8967-5 (hc)
ISBN: 978-1-4907-8969-9 (e)

Library of Congress Control Number: 2018950634

Trafford rev. 08/03/2018

Trafford PUBLISHING® www.trafford.com
North America & international
toll-free: 1 888 232 4444 (USA & Canada)
fax: 812 355 4082

Permissions

Cover design by Michele Edington

To Sam Deibler,
Gordon Gibson, and
David Tomkinson.

I have shared my journey of the spirit with them for over a half century.

I also write this with deep appreciation for the Unitarian Universalist congregations I have served since 1979. It is for them I originally prepared much of the material contained herein in the form of the sermons I delivered.

Thanks for listening!

When we are stunned beyond words we are finally starting to get somewhere.

—Anne Lamott

CONTENTS

FOREWORD

[T]here is something sacred or holy contained within the ordinary or the everyday, and if we stay open to it that sacredness or holiness will, on occasion, break through. (From the text).

A box full of Tinkertoys is scattered on the floor in front of you. Such is the jumble of this life. Some of the pieces are days or months or seconds, some hot dogs or kids' soccer games or parent-teacher conferences or serotonin. What isn't there on the floor is the bigger stuff, such as meaning or purpose or God or grace, because we must construct these for ourselves. Not that they don't really exist on their own—that's a bigger question than what I'm prepared to take on here. But we don't have any connection to them until we do the work of assembling them, and this work, the putting together of the pieces, is the nearest we get to living them. People often talk about trying to find meaning or find God, but this is like trying to find a car or a pyramid in a box of Tinkertoys. You can get to the thing you want, but you have to create it.

This means we have a lot of leeway in how we construct meaning or purpose or holiness in our lives. All the variations that a thinking person can go through over a lifetime—trying first this architecture then that—would fill a book.

What follows is that book.

If you are hoping to find meaning or God among the rods and spools herein, I can spare you some trouble. What you will find instead is mystery and some tools you might use in tackling this mystery for yourself. What's most permanent—and maybe what's most holy—is the *process* of trying to get there and our willingness to mess with what we thought was perfection to create something just a little better.

Steve Edington begins this book's journey as an unlikely candidate to tackle this mystery. As the son of a southern West Virginian Baptist deacon, he "received Jesus" at age eleven and got his call to ministry at age thirteen, with a clear blueprint of how the pieces of life fit together. But instead of camping in this solid edifice, he embarks on a journey of enlightenment not found in the hymnals. He once was found, but now he's lost—keenly attuned to the mystery of the wilderness enveloping him. If you're going through hell, as the saying goes, you better keep going. But if you're going through the woods around Walden Pond, you're probably better off sitting and thinking a while. Knowing that you're lost is the point. You may not get to the bottom of the mystery, but on a good day the pondering is holiness enough.

And on a great day, you'll find some guides to help with this pondering. Dante had his Beatrice; the Reverend Steve Edington, on his way to and through the Unitarian Universalist ministry, calls on a different cast of sages, including Rabindranath Tagore, *Doonesbury*, Joni Mitchell, gestalt therapy, William James, Marcus Borg, the New York Mets, Ralph Waldo Emerson, Thich Nhat Hanh, and Iris DeMent. It is Ms. DeMent who provides the book's last word, far from the evangelical Baptist pulpit where the journey began—"I think I'll just let mystery be." To these wise guides, readers can add Steve Edington.

As for mystery, he reminds us that we can view it as an affront or a delight, approach it "with resignation or anticipation." In each pairing, the latter term wants to unite us in process, the former to divide us in product. In this book, religion—"the search for that which ultimately binds our lives together, for what gives them wholeness"—is a verb.

Edington is a formidable Beat Generation scholar and a director of the annual Lowell (Massachusetts) Celebrates Kerouac festivals. It is possible to look at *God Is Not God's Name: A Journey beyond Words* as a road book, leading away from a fixed belief toward a more open-ended questioning. The journey is Edington's, but not his alone. As in other road books, including Kerouac's, for all the answers it poses to life's important questions, it recognizes that the answers are transitory or provisional, and the questions permanent. They'll be around, and pilgrims will still be puzzling over them, long after these pages have crumbled to dust or magnetic noise.

I think the author has a few more chapters yet to write, but that's the nature of Tinkertoys: we use impermanent, endlessly changeable materials to give shape to what we call eternal forms.

Until then, if we can be kinder in our answers, more grateful for mystery, better attuned to the creative impulse that goes into constructing an answer, less sure of the answer itself, more forgiving of our and others' failures, we will be practicing religion as a verb.

We will do so no matter what nouns we use—or what names we create for this thing called God—to keep the Tinkertoys in order.

John Leland

John Leland is a feature writer for The New York Times. *He is the author of* Hip: The History, Why Kerouac Matters: The Lessons of "On the Road," *and* Happiness Is a Choice You Make.

PREFACE

Full disclosure right at the outset: the title of this book is a straight steal from a very fine human being whom I was blessed to know for a number of years, the late Rev. Dr. F. Forrester Church.

Forrest, as he was generally known, served the Unitarian Church of All Souls in New York City for thirty-one years until his very untimely death at the age of sixty-one from esophageal cancer. He was the son of the late United States Senator Frank Church of Idaho.

Reverend Church was one of the more literate and prolific spokespersons for the liberal religion in America in the late twentieth and early twenty-first centuries. Contained within the fourteen books he published during his lifetime were a number of short-take gems, including "God is not God's name. It is a name for that which is greater than all and present in all."

As I read them, these two rather simple lines take the whole belief-in-God conversation to a much more productive, meaningful, and promising place than one of going in circles over whether or not one believes in an entity called "God." They get us out of the semantic box over who or what God is or may be. They take us beyond endless debates over the existence or nonexistence of a Supreme Being.

Instead, they call us into a spiritual journey or a quest for our discovering, if only in part, "that which is greater than all and present in all." If one chooses to call the object of that quest "God," fine. If not, it's equally fine. In the end, it doesn't matter. Whatever beliefs, perspectives, philosophies, or life stances any of us may come to, and however much they may change and evolve over the course of our lifetimes, it is wired into our human hard drives to look beyond ourselves for some greater meaning or purpose in our lives beyond the rubrics of our earthly existence.

This point is well made by Dr. Huston Smith in his book *Why Religion Matters*:

> There is within us—even in the blithest, most lighthearted of us—a fundamental disease. It acts like an unquenchable fire that renders the vast majority of us incapable in this life of ever coming to full peace. The desire lives in the marrow of our bones and in the deep regions of our souls. All great literature, poetry, art, and philosophy try to name or analyze this longing. We are seldom in direct touch with it, and indeed the modern world seems set on preventing us from getting in touch with it . . . But the longing is there; built into us like a jack-in-the-box that presses for release.

The "disease" to which Dr. Smith refers is not a physical ailment or a mental illness. He is referring to a spiritual condition and is using the term in its most literal sense: dis-ease. He is referring to an ongoing—and not always conscious—uneasiness within us that we may be missing something with respect to what life and living can be. It is a sense, again consciously or not, of a disconnect among some of the more unfulfilled portions of our lives and the greater fullness of living to which we aspire. Even if we cannot adequately define or identify what this greater fullness might be, we still long for it. All our great literature, poetry, art, philosophy, and religion, as Smith notes, are ultimately rooted in our desire and in our attempts to attend to this uneasiness or disconnect that generates our longing.

For all of Dr. Smith's wisdom, it was a first-century Jewish prophet whom we know by the name of Jesus of Nazareth who said the same thing in a much more succinct way: "Life is more than bread, and the body more than clothing."

Once we attend to our basic survival needs (food, clothing, shelter, etc.), this is what we come to—a need for an assurance or at least for some hope or possibility that life is more than bread, more than our physical existence, that is to say. Indeed, the spiritual quest is an ongoing attempt to reach this often elusive "more than."

I am not an anthropologist, but I would maintain that the point in human evolution at which proto-human beings became *Homo sapiens* occurred when our pre-human ancestors found enough of a respite from their immediate survival needs and were able to look up and then look around and then look at themselves and begin to wonder why. This was also the stage at which our earliest human ancestors' brains had developed to the point where they could begin to ask—even in the vaguest and most seminal of ways—ultimate questions of existence.

A mythological account of this stage in human evolution is right there in one of the creation narratives found in the opening chapters of Genesis. The proto-humans, given the names Adam and Eve, had this defining and humanizing moment: "The eyes of both of them were opened and they discovered they were naked" (Genesis 3:7 NEB).

This passage is not about a couple of mythological creatures seeing each other's bodies—as well as their own—for the first time and then trying to get themselves under wraps. It is instead a fanciful recounting of when our earliest human ancestors first achieved self-awareness—that is, "their eyes were opened" and they beheld themselves. This was an emerging self-awareness that in time came to include the knowledge of their mortality. And that, I would submit, was also the beginning of religion. This gets me back to my dearly departed friend and colleague Forrest Church and another of his gems. "Religion," he wrote, "is our human response to the dual reality of being alive and knowing we will die." It is in response to what Forrest called this "dual reality" that we search for "that which is greater than all and present in all."

I guess it's inevitable that we try to affix some name to this greater reality that we all, in one way or another, seek after. My point here is that whatever name we may come up with is a secondary consideration. A stumbling block we often encounter when we use the term *God* in this process is that we get sidetracked into defending our use of a term rather than remaining on a course of discovery about what it is that gives our lives their ultimate meaning and value. This is not to suggest that we get rid of the word *God*. Since that's never going to happen, any such suggestion is pointless. What I'm offering here is a cautionary tale about not letting a word, whether we choose to use it or not, get in our way when it comes to our seeking and finding spiritual depth in our lives.

In telling this tale, I'll be bringing some of my own story into it. What follows in the pages ahead is a combination of spiritual autobiography and some of the religious, spiritual, and basic life conclusions I've come to at this point in my life. I write this as I begin to wind down a forty-year ministry in the liberal religious tradition—in my case as a Unitarian Universalist parish minister. It's time to sum some things up while my mind and spirit are still—I hope—active enough to do the summing.

My story has its origins in southern West Virginia where some of my earliest memories include standing on a pew in a Baptist church and singing, "O happy day, O happy day, when Jesus washed my sins away." I had no idea what I was singing about as a five-year-old, but it felt right.

From there, the story wound its way around a call to the ministry when I was thirteen. The minister of the evangelical Baptist church where I was raised was the first person I encountered whom I wanted to be like when I grew up, so it made sense that he was the first person I told about my calling. Religiously and theologically speaking, I've ended up light-years away from this humble and quiet-spoken individual who has long since passed on. But his support and encouragement of me during a very fragile and formative time in my life is something for which I ever remain indebted.

Still, I'm amazed, when I think about it, as I write these words now in the early years of the eighth decade of my life, that my call to ministry has remained intact. To be sure, as I've hinted, the meaning of the call has gone through some pretty radical redefining over the decades. But I've never been able to shake it off, and I've long given up trying.

Contained within those decades are eight years of college and theological school, during which I moved from the right wing to the left wing—theologically speaking—of Protestant Christianity and took ordination in a mainline, liberal Protestant denomination. Then there was an excursion into what was called the human potential movement and my dabbling in humanistic psychology. This got me into an atheist or agnostic (I never could decide which) period that even made my liberal Christian ordination vows a bit, shall we say, shaky.

Wherever my mind may have been going, I remained unable to get my ministerial identity out of my gut. And in time, I found a spiritual home in the Unitarian Universalist ministry. The term *spiritual home* may be misleading. It does not mean that I arrived at a final destination but rather that I have found a reliable point of departure from which I could continue the journey.

The greatest gift I've been given in my years in the liberal religious ministry has also proven to be its greatest challenge. I carry the awareness that those with whom I minister are looking to me for spiritual guidance and, in Forrest's words once again, for my direction in their search for "that which is greater than all and present in all." Knowing this, I feel both a challenge and a demand to ever remain on my own journey of discovery.

That's the view, then, from thirty thousand feet of nearly eight decades of living and exploring. I'll put the wheels on the ground from time to time in the pages ahead. Mine, of course, is only one story. Any of those who read on will bring their own stories to the text. As varied as our stories may be, what we share in common is what Huston Smith called the desire that lives "in the marrow of our bones and in the deep regions of our souls."

We can name the object of that desire by any term we may choose—"God" or otherwise. What I seek to do here is move beyond a name toward whatever truths it may point us.

Finally, I concede the irony of writing a book with the words *beyond words* in its subtitle. If I were to truly go beyond words, the following pages would all be blank! I am hardly the first to deal with this conundrum, however. Jewish scholars tell us that in the aftermath of the Babylonian exile of the sixth century BCE, the Jews ceased to use their name for God—Yahweh—because the divine name had come to be regarded as too sacred and holy to even be spoken. They had to come up with other ways to identify what they regarded as ultimately sacred and holy. I can relate.

Chapter 1

The Belief Trap

One of the rewarding, and at the same time sobering, aspects of being in the ministry is the entrée a minister is granted into the deeper regions of human lives.

One such entrée granted to me was with a young man we'll call Charles. He came to see me because he was enraged at God. He had no ties to the church I was serving, and we'd never met until he came in for his scheduled appointment. He attended one of the Alcoholics Anonymous groups that met weekly at the church and had seen my name listed as its minister.

Charles had spent several years caring on a round-the-clock basis for his very ill mother who was slowly dying from a debilitating disease of the nervous system. To help make expenses meet (since Charles had to give up his job to care for his mother) and pay the medical bills that insurance didn't cover, his elderly and semiretired father had to take on extra jobs. Now his mother is dead, his father is exhausted and has been denied much of what could have been a good retirement, and Charles is angry. He is angry at the God in whom he sincerely and devoutly believes.

Charles, as already indicated, is a recovering alcoholic. A personal and intentional Supreme Being God is his higher power. This is the God who, as Charles sees it, has been keeping him sober, even through the most difficult and devastating period of his life. We talk. The anger flows forth. But in the midst of the anger is a deep-seated fear—a fear of what will happen if Charles lets his anger at God overtake his need for God. When I try as gently as I can to get the conversation around to the idea of reimagining God in such a way that would involve letting go of the notion of a God who would cause his mother to suffer and die in the manner that she did, it doesn't work. To go that route, as Charles sees it, would mean losing the higher power, or God, who is keeping him sober. And neither he nor I want him backsliding into active alcoholism.

I have to admit—to myself at least—that there is a certain logic to Charles's way of thinking. Charles has put God in charge of his life, and God, in turn, is keeping him sober. This is how Charles understands his quid pro quo arrangement with God: I turn my life over to You, and You keep me sober because You are the one who is ultimately in charge of my life as well as all life in general. So he quite logically asks, "Isn't the God who is in charge of my life the God who is, or was, in charge of my mother's life until recently? It's the same God isn't it? How am I supposed to hate the God who is keeping me clean and sober?" I can't risk alienating "Him" after all. But the hatred is there; and Charles's anger at God, coupled with his need for God, is tearing him apart.

I hesitate to turn Charles into a "type" because his specific and painful situation was hardly what one would call typical. But his predicament, in a much broader sense, and in a way that transcends the tragedy and frustration and anger he's feeling, typifies, I feel, the modern predicament when it comes to belief. That predicament, simply put, is wanting or needing to believe in a God who is not always believable.

What I didn't say in our conversations, because the time did not feel right for it, was that the problem we were contending with was not about "God" as such but with Charles's way of believing in God. Unfortunately, the conversation did not make it to that point because after just a few visits, Charles ended our brief encounter. I do not know how he resolved his dilemma or if he ever did. I can only hope that Charles has come to some measure of personal peace and has found some spiritual comfort by whatever means he may have sought them.

I use this incident to set the stage for this chapter as I think on the conversation I would have liked to have had with Charles had we continued. He had gotten himself caught in what I'm calling the *belief trap*, that is to say, being so locked in to a particular way of believing in

God that he could not envision any other alternatives that might have served him better than the way of believing he was clinging to.

Perhaps Charles and I could have opened with "What does 'belief in God' even mean?" Is it belief in a Supreme Being who oversees and intervenes in the workings of nature and in human affairs? Is it Someone, with a capital *S*, who is in charge of everything and whose interventions we can seek through prayer? Is this a God who, in the soothing words my devoutly religious father used to sing to me when I was a child, "walks with me and talks with me and tells me I am his own"? A lot of belief in God stems from a real human need—the need to feel that Someone, again with a capital *S*, is in charge. Indeed, it can be very comforting to have a Someone who knows and cares about us and—if need be—keeps us sober. "His eye is on the sparrow, and I know He watches me," as another soothing song from my youthful days put it.

But a God who can act in purposeful ways and cause things to happen can also create problems when it comes to one's faith formation. He, She, or It (pick your pronoun) can become a God we have to rationalize about when a tragedy strikes or when some of life's injustices and terrible cruelties come our way. But that's not God, the traditional theist says. God is the one who gives us the strength to deal with such adversities. But sometimes these kinds of rationalizations that are, in a sense, apologies for God just plain give out. Charles came to see me because he could no longer do that kind of rationalizing. He could no longer hold the two together: the God who was keeping him sober and the God who caused his mother to suffer until she died. For him, they were one and the same.

As something of a counterpoint to Charles, I recall a former parishioner of one of the churches I served whom I'll call Mike. Mike's college-age daughter was brutally murdered by a supposed "boyfriend" in her college dormitory. While her memorial service was one of the most difficult I've ever planned and officiated, my difficulty was absolutely nothing compared to the incomprehensible anguish the parents of this young woman, who were divorced, experienced.

I had no contact with the mother outside of planning the service. It was her father Mike who came to me when he got the news. One of the first things he said to me when we sat to talk in the same room where Charles and I had had our conversations was "At least I'm glad I don't believe in an intentional God because I'd sure be angry at the evil son of a bitch!" Mike had all the grief and anger he could handle as it was, and he found at least some small measure of relief in that he didn't have to take anything out on God.

But God does not cause tragedy and cruelty and horrible losses one may protest. And I absolutely agree. I agree because I do not believe in a Supreme Being who "causes" anything—good, bad, or indifferent. I am willing to believe that more people become atheists over this idea of a God who "causes things" than for any other reason. So when it comes to my own voyage of faith and to my own pursuit of "that which is greater than all and present in all," the first thing that gets tossed overboard is a God who causes things. And the second thing that gets tossed over is a Supreme Being with any kind of a will or intent.

The God I tossed over, somewhere back there in my humanistic psychology phase, is the God that Richard Dawkins takes on and sets about debunking in his book *The God Delusion.* He says so right in his first chapter where he posits what he calls the *God hypothesis* that he sets forth as "a superhuman, supernatural intelligence who deliberately designed and created the universe and everything in it, including us." He goes on, "God, in this sense defined, is a delusion." He then continues on for nearly four hundred pages in explaining why the God he has so defined is a delusion.

Ironic as it may sound, I found Dawkins's book to be of scarcely any value to me in my own journey of faith and spirit because I agreed with practically all of it. I also found a certain kind of intellectual dishonesty about it in that Dr. Dawkins puts God in a belief box of his (Dawkins's) own construction, blows up the box, and then claims he's dealt with the whole "God question." After all, it's easy to debunk a hypothesis when you are the one who creates the hypothesis you want to debunk!

I can imagine Dawkins's reply to me would be that he didn't create the God Hypothesis he cited all on his own or out of thin air. It is an understanding of God that is held by millions, if not billions, of believers professing a wide variety of faiths all over the world. I can concede that argument while still holding that the term *God* cannot be reduced to any one single hypothesis, however widely held such a hypothesis may be. If God is not God's name, then casting off one way of appropriating that name may be of some help in one's faith journey, but it hardly brings the journey to a halt.

Another irony I find in Dawkins's work is that rather than positing a conclusion to a journey of faith, he offers instead a beginning. He clears the forest, so to speak, of traditional, supernatural theism—that is, the belief in a Supreme Being with a will and an intent—so that other possible paths through the forest may be explored. It is, apparently, Dawkins's choice not to explore them. Be that as it may, such exploration begins and is moved along by the longing and the yearning to which Huston Smith refers in this book's introduction. It is a yearning or longing that persists, regardless of how many belief boxes one may cast aside. To come at it from the reverse angle, it is a yearning or longing that cannot be completely extinguished however devoutly attached one may become to a particular set of beliefs. To think otherwise, as I see it, is to fall into the belief trap.

While Dr. Smith describes this longing in admirable and well-crafted language, I find a more on-the-ground expression of it in some of the writings of the late John Updike, his four "Rabbit" novels in particular. These four books, written over the course of thirty years, cover the life of Harry "Rabbit" Angstrom. Harry is Updike's everyman. He owns and operates an automobile dealership in the fictitious town of Brewer, Pennsylvania, for which Updike's hometown of Shillington, Pennsylvania, provides the prototype. Harry's glory days were as a high school basketball star where he was known for darting around the court like, well, a rabbit. Now he's just a guy with a wife and a kid, trying to make a living while also vaguely and largely inarticulately trying to figure out what else there is to life besides being a guy who is trying to make it through life.

Updike gives his everyman the surname of "Angstrom" as a play on the German-derived word *angst.* While a precise definition of this term is elusive, it generally refers to a kind of nameless anxiety or foreboding or even dread. In Harry's case it comes off as an undefined longing, a sense that he is missing something without even knowing what this intangible "something" is. Some of Harry's nameless longing is mixed in with the memories of his glory days on the basketball court when he knew he was somebody who amounted to something. With that vaunted identity gone, he is only left to wonder.

In the first of the Rabbit novels, *Rabbit, Run*, which is set in the early 1960s, Harry is a young adult facing the various adult realities of most white middle-class Americans of that era. He is not a churchgoer, but his spiritual angst leads him to seek the counsel of the local Episcopal minister Reverend Eccles (another Updike word play, this one with "ecclesiastical"). Instead of attending his church services, Harry becomes Reverend Eccles's golfing buddy. Their trips to, from, and on the golf course provide the settings for their conversations where Harry unburdens some of his angst onto Reverend Eccles, which the good Reverend tries to address in whatever ways he can.

One of my favorite passages in the annals of American literature is Updike's description of a ride Harry and Reverend Eccles take to one of their golf games, with Harry speaking in response to some spiritual counsel Reverend Eccles has attempted to offer.

> "Well, I don't know about all this theology, but I'll tell you, I do feel, I guess, that somewhere behind all this"—Harry gestures outward at the scenery; they are passing the housing development this side of the golf course, half-wood, half-brick one-and-a half stories in little flat bull-dozed yards holding tricycles and spindly three-year-old trees—"there is something that wants me to find it."

That passage provides one of the underpinnings of Updike's four Rabbit novels as Harry seeks this elusive "something that wants me to find it." Updike takes his readers through this ordinary guy's life with its ups and downs in the latter half of twentieth-century middle-class America, with his protagonist trying to make some greater sense of it all. The closest Harry came to such fulfillment—the closest he got to "God" one might say—was on his high school basketball court. So it makes for a certain symmetry that the final Rabbit novel, *Rabbit at Rest*, ends with an aging Harry Angstrom, who is now a grandfather, dying of a heart attack in a one-on-one game of basketball with a young African American fellow, some fifty years his junior.

If you make your way through all the Rabbit novels what you get in the character of Harry Angstrom is a life lived in the absence of some higher unifying meaning or purpose, a life that does not quite make a connection to—in Dr. Church's language again—"that which is greater than all and present in all." Or if you prefer, Harry's is a life lived in the absence of God. This does not mean Harry's life is completely barren. It isn't one devoid of any sort of earthly meaning or purpose. Harry does well enough for himself and lives a decent enough life, even with his occasional infidelities. (Updike could not have written all he did if he couldn't have written, sometimes in rather graphic detail, of sexual infidelities.) It's just that Harry's life never quite reaches the fullness to which he aspires, or the glory he had known, on the basketball court.

It is time to leave Harry to his rest. Having done so, we're still left with the longing that Huston Smith and John Updike, each in their own way, describe. Where to go with it then? One thing to do early on is to acknowledge this chapter's title—the belief trap. The belief trap, simply put, is the idea that this longing can be fully addressed or at least adequately met by subscribing to a prescribed set of beliefs. The more strongly or vehemently I hear someone—usually a religious fundamentalist of one stripe or another—insist that they possess "the truth," the more I suspect or am convinced that they're really afraid, on some level, that they don't. They have convinced themselves of the rightness of their particular and usually very narrowly focused brand of religion as a way of avoiding or denying the longing that remains in the depths of their souls. Such is the belief trap.

After giving due heed to the belief trap, the next step is to make peace with this longing or yearning. Living a life of honest seeking means you'll never fully escape the longing—deal with it. After all, as Dr. Smith rightly points out, much of our great literature, art, poetry, and philosophy are inspired by and originated from this longing. Use your longing then as a prod to your own voyages of faith and spirit. Just because you may never reach a final port or destination does not mean that the trip itself cannot be an exciting and fulfilling one. So bon voyage; just don't go thinking you've ever fully and finally arrived at whatever port you may occasionally pull into.

When it comes to my voyage, what has come for me after pulling free of the belief trap is a willingness to live with Mystery—Mystery with a capital *M*. There are two ways one can live in such a fashion: with resignation or with anticipation.

Resignation is to take the stance that since there is no final port of call where all becomes revealed and known about what gives life its ultimate meaning, then why bother at all? Finding a comforting and well-delineated set of beliefs is one antidote to this resignation. This works quite well for any number of people, and far be it from me to deny them access to their antidote—even if I could, and I know I can't.

I choose anticipation—to live in the midst of Mystery while remaining open to hints of the sacred or the divine as contained within the ordinary or even the banal, even as banal as "little flat bulldozed yards with spindly three-year-old trees." There's a ten-dollar sounding word for this kind of anticipation called *panenthesim*. It is not posed as yet another stab at a definition of God, so much as it is a life stance, a way of looking at and living life. As I've come to understand the term (without, I hope, getting too overly invested in it), it is a meaningful or at least hopeful way of living in the midst of Mystery.

Panentheism offers a particular way of encountering the world where we live. It is a mind-set that allows us to see life in a certain way. It is not a stance we can continually maintain but one we enter into now and then. Panentheism holds that there is something of the sacred or the holy contained not only in the ordinary but also in the fallen and broken places of life. And if we can stay open to it—if we can live with anticipation in the midst of Mystery—sacredness will occasionally break through.

There is a passage in the writings of the Hindu poet and philosopher Rabindranath Tagore that describes what I would call a panentheistic moment. I do not know the particular experience to which he is referring, but these are his words: "I suddenly felt as if some ancient mist had been lifted from my sight and the ultimate significance of all things laid bare . . . and no person or thing in the world seemed trivial or unpleasing." That, I feel, is what it truly means to realize life—to see no person or thing in the world as trivial. From the standpoint of panentheism, Tagore is describing a "God moment". You may call it what you will; the experience is far more important than the name. Such a stance has little, if anything, to do with embracing a set of beliefs; rather it is about maintaining a stance of openness in the midst of Mystery to the gifts of the Spirit that can come our way.

This is not a standpoint that will protect one from life's tragedies, pain, horrible losses, and terrible absurdities. There is no God in panentheism for one to get angry or enraged at. Instead, this is a perspective for keeping faith with life in the midst of its blessings as well as its curses.

I referred above to the phrase "realize life." I take it from yet another of my favorite literary passages. In this case, it is the third act of Thornton Wilder's play *Our Town.* It's a scene that brings me close to tears whenever I read or see it.

From Broadway to local community theaters, *Our Town* is probably one of the most often produced plays in America. It has to do with the comings and goings of the town of Grover's Corners, New Hampshire, which Wilder patterned after the town of Peterborough, New Hampshire, which happens to be just a short distance west from where I live. The activities of Grover's Corners are overseen by an omniscient Stage Manager who supplies a narrative thread while also interacting now and then with the characters. He is a one-man Greek chorus.

One of the play's story lines is the developing relationship between young George Gibbs and his girlfriend Emily Webb, which eventually results in their marriage. The third act takes place after Emily Gibbs dies while giving birth to her and George's second child when she is twenty-six years old. Emily's character remains in the play, however, since the third act takes place in the cemetery up on a hill overlooking the town. Here the deceased have the cemetery all to themselves, and they can converse with one another while looking down upon the town where most of them spent their lives.

The State Manager, who is something of a godlike figure, can also go up to the cemetery and join in the conversation. This is just what he does in the third act.

As the cemetery scene unfolds, the Stage Manager tells the recently deceased Emily that she is allowed to see or revisit from her postlife perspective any day of her life that she wants. The other deceased souls tell her not to do it, but Emily cannot resist and asks to see the day of her twelfth birthday again.

She remembers it as being a very special day in her life, the time when she was just on the verge of womanhood. But when she is allowed to see it again from the angle she now has, knowing all that will come afterward until her death fourteen years later, she experiences mostly sadness and even anguish because what she sees is how taken for granted and routine everything is. She realizes how precious, and how sacred even, so much of life is and how human beings—herself included from when she was a human being—mostly miss it while going about the various and sundry tasks of their lives.

Her lament is that people do not really look at one another when they have the chance to so do. They do not fully touch, and they do not fully experience the depth of life that is all around them—even in as pedantic a place as an ordinary American town. From her postlife place, Emily tries to talk to her mother as she views the events of her twelfth birthday: "Just for a moment now, we're all together. Mama, just for a moment, we're happy. Let's really look at one another."

Of course, neither her mother nor anyone else can hear Emily now. The deceased Emily quickly recognizes this and tells the Stage Manager she's seen enough, and the replay of her twelfth birthday comes to an end. As the scene ends, Emily delivers these lines to herself, to the Stage Manager and to the other departed folks she's recently joined: "It goes so fast. We don't have time to look at one another. I didn't realize. So all that was going on and we never noticed . . . O Earth, you are too wonderful for anyone to realize you . . ."

And then directly to the State Manager, she asks, "Do any human beings ever realize life while they live it—every, every minute?" The Stage Manager replies, "No." And then after a pause, he adds, "The saints and poets—maybe they do some."

Wilder's Stage Manager, as Wilder's voice, is clearly right when he says that we human beings do not realize life "every, every minute." I take no issue with that. But I like to think and believe that there is just enough of the saint or poet in us that we really can—if only at certain holy moments—look at one another and realize life as we live it. I live with the hope that we can do that at least enough times and in enough ways to let us know that we are in the midst of something precious and sacred and holy, as well as something very fragile, that is only ours to hold for a time.

And so it is as we live in the Mystery that surrounds and enfolds us.

I give the last word here to the singer and songwriter Iris DeMent:

> Everybody's wonderin' what and where they all came from
> Everybody's worryin' 'bout where they're going to go
> When the whole thing's done.
> But no one knows for certain,
> And so it's all the same to me
> I'll think I'll just let the mystery be . . .
>
> I believe in love, and I live my life accordingly,
> But I choose to let the mystery be.

Chapter 2

Belief versus the Religious Impulse

Beliefs come and go; religion remains. I probably knew that by the time I reached the age of thirty. But this chapter of my life from that time brought it home for me:

In the mid-1970s, I was cruising along in and out of my religious and spiritual ports of call. The near fundamentalism of the evangelical Baptist church of my upbringing was well in the rearview mirror, thanks in good measure to my college years. I could still identify certain positive aspects from both of those settings to carry along with me, taking what still worked and discarding what didn't. College immediately led into theological school. The call to ministry I'd heard at age thirteen was still in play. My latter years of college, along with the liberal, mainline Protestant seminary I attended, had radically redefined what ministry meant for me from when I was thirteen, but I was staying the course as far as the ministry itself went.

I was a few years out of seminary after being ordained in a fairly liberal large American Baptist church in a suburb of Rochester, New York, following my graduation from the Colgate Rochester Divinity School. My ordination review committee had let me skate by some of the trickier matters, such as the physical resurrection of Jesus or the virgin birth, by not asking me about them. I was, after all, a "promising young minister," so why mess things up? Fresh out of seminary, I somehow managed to land a position as an interdenominational university campus minister supported by a consortium of several mainline Protestant bodies. For those who read Garry Trudeau's *Doonesbury* comic strip, I refer to that period in my life as my "Rev. Scot Sloan Days."

Personally, I was hanging pretty loose. I'd already chalked one marriage and divorce. While no divorce is pain-free, my first wife and I at least had the wherewithal to end the marriage without any children to create custody issues for us, and we'd acquired no money or property worth contending over. So it was just me, my apartment in Stevens Point, Wisconsin, and the programs I was generating and running for an organization called United Ministries in Higher Education on the University of Wisconsin—Stevens Point campus.

Since campus activity geared down over the summer and as I had no family responsibilities to attend to, I headed off to San Francisco and Berkeley in the summers of '75 and '76 to dip my toe in what was called the human-potential movement. In my case, this involved taking part in a series of gestalt therapy workshops and seminars led by disciples of Fritz Perls. That's another story all by itself. Suffice it to say here I had a good time hanging out with some rather crazy people who were still quite loveable in their own weird ways.

But what came out of that experience was some real soul-searching for me. I had to face up to the truth that my spiritual odyssey was taking me beyond even the most liberalized interpretations of Christianity. Since no one was giving me any kind of doctrinal checkup, I knew I could stay with my campus ministry position for as long as I wished. But with all the exposure I'd just had to the necessity of personal authenticity, I still had to ask myself if I could continue in good faith and conscience to represent a variety of mainline Protestant denominations, even as a liberal Christian. The answer was no. The beliefs I'd professed, even to the most accommodating of ordination review boards, were no longer holding up.

This story has a few more twists and turns that I'll touch on later. Most significantly, it includes a remarriage that, I'm pleased and blessed to say, has lasted to this day and will presumably continue for the remainder of my days. To cut to the chase for now, nearly three years after leaving my campus ministry position in Stevens Point, I was serving a small and delightful Unitarian Universalist congregation in the coastal town of

Rockland, Maine. My wife, Michele, got a job—can't make this up—as the office manager for a lobster company.

What kept me in the ministry then? It was a matter of quite literally going beyond belief. I found that while I could discard certain beliefs that no longer sustained me or that even made a lot of sense, I could not shake off religion or the religious impulse. Religion, that is to say, in the sense of my late friend Forrest Church's definition as "our human response to the dual reality of being alive and knowing that we will die." Or to put it another way, religion is our human attempt to make some ultimate sense out of the lives we are living, even as we know we'll never fully get there. It's still worth the journey, however elusive the final destination may be.

I've found in the Unitarian Universalist ministry a place that allows me to be a religious leader with these kinds of understandings of what being a "religious leader" means. It has given me a place where being a religious leader (a designation I seriously take) does not mean I've got "the truth" that I then impart to my followers. It's a place, instead, where I am a fellow traveler bringing whatever wisdom, knowledge, and experience I may have gained over the course of my years to those who are on the journey with me. I have shared the knowledge, wisdom, and experiences that have come my way as best I can, with the congregations that have called me to walk with them.

For all the beliefs I've discarded, going back to the evangelical Baptist church of my childhood and adolescence, I continue to believe in the religious impulse. One of the more poignant expressions I've found of this impulse is a meditation by the late Rev. Ralph Helverson titled "Impassioned Clay." It is a poetic version of Huston Smith's more academic treatment of the subject.

Impassioned Clay

Deep in ourselves resides the religious impulse.
Out of the passions of our clay it rises.
We have religion when we stop deluding ourselves that we are self-sufficient, self-sustaining, or self-derived.
We have religion when we hold some hope beyond the present,
Some self-respect beyond our failures.

> We have religion when our hearts are capable of leaping up at beauty,
> When our nerves are edged by some dream in our heart.
> We have religion when we have an abiding gratitude for all that we have received.
> We have religion when we look upon people with all their failings
> And still find in them good.
> We have religion when we look beyond people to the grandeur of nature
> And to the purpose in our own heart.
> We have religion when we have done all we can,
> And then in confidence trust ourselves to the life that is
> Larger than ourselves.

For me, that last line best captures what the religious impulse is. It is about looking up from our individual states of existence to a life that is, as Helverson puts it, "larger than ourselves" and in which we feel some trust and confidence. To put it another way, the religious impulse is the drive to feel at home in a universe that still remains greatly mysterious to us and that fills us with awe and wonder and, occasionally, fear.

It's caveat time. I am well aware of the terrible, horrible, no good, very bad (thank you Judith Viorst) ways in which religion gets used. We can make that abused. My knowledge of world history is sufficient for me to know the wars that have been fought, the tortures that have been inflicted, and the executions that have taken place in the supposed name of religion.

In a somewhat less brutal but still unconscionable manner, I am aware of how religion can be manipulated to foster useless guilt and to rationalize all manner of repression and wrongdoing. I am aware of how religion can provide a means for self-aggrandizement on the part of any number of "holy hucksters" who are able to convince enough of their willing followers that they possess the whole truth. The horrific and unfathomable mass suicides at Jonestown, Guyana, done at the behest of Rev. Jim Jones in November of 1978 provide an example of this horrible phenomenon.

A debate over whether religion is a force for good or for evil can be of value when it comes to gaining a better understanding of how those conflicting forces operate. At the same time, it's a debate that is never fully resolved because there is no final resolution. The contention by some well-intentioned people that the world would be a much better place without religion—cue up John Lennon here: "and no religion too"—does not, in the end, hold up. Religion exists because human beings exist and have within them the religious impulse that Huston Smith and Ralph Helverson well describe. And while that impulse can be put to all kinds of destructive ends, it is ultimately life-enhancing, provided it is responded to in life-enhancing ways.

And yes, there are certain beliefs or life stances that can help us meaningfully respond to this religious impulse. I'll address some of them in the chapters that follow this one. But part of the belief trap—as referred to in the previous chapter—is the notion that a given set of precisely delineated beliefs can fully and adequately address this religious impulse. It is this notion, in fact, that lies at the heart of many of the abusive, exploitative, and manipulative ways in which religion is used.

But rather than go on with all the negative effects of the attempts to reduce the religious impulse to an exclusive set of beliefs, let's try some humor. While cruising the Internet for some sermon material several years ago, I came across a comedic category for the "best God joke ever." I found it on a website called Ship of Fools, which is a liberal Christian outfit that mostly pokes fun at some of the more extreme expressions of Christianity, as well as religion in general.

The "joke" is actually a stand-up comedy routine done by a Chicago-based comedian named Emo Philips. There are several versions and variations on it floating around. This is the original version as done and preferred by Mr. Philips:

(Another caveat: Suicide is a terribly serious matter. I've dealt with enough families and loved ones of suicide victims as well as those contemplating suicide to know this all too well. And I can still appreciate the point Mr. Philips is making in this very humorous schtick.)

> I was in San Francisco walking over the Golden Gate Bridge, and I saw a man about to jump.
> I said, "Don't jump! God loves you."
> He said, "He does?"
> I said, "Of course He does. Are you a Christian or a Jew?"
> He said, "A Christian."
> I said, "Me too! Protestant or Catholic?"
> He said, "Protestant."
> I said, "Me too! What franchise?"
> He said, "Baptist."
> I said, "Me too! Northern Baptist or Southern Baptist?"
> He said, "Northern Baptist."
> I said, "Me too! Northern Fundamentalist Baptist or Northern Reformed?"
> He said, "Northern Fundamentalist Baptist."
> I said, "Me too! Northern Fundamentalist Baptist Great Lakes Conference, or Northern Fundamentalist Baptist Eastern Seaboard?"
> He said, "Northern Fundamentalist Baptist Great Lakes Conference."
> I said, "Me too! Northern Fundamentalist Baptist Great Lakes Regional Conference, Council of 1879, or Northern Fundamentalist Baptist Great Lakes Conference, Council of 1912?"
> He said, "Northern Fundamentalist Baptist Great Lakes Conference, Council of 1912."
> I said, "'Die, heretic!" And I pushed him over!

I still have to stop and laugh every time I read that. Like most good comedy or satire, this bit has a bite to it, having to do with the absurd lengths to which matters of religious belief can be taken. The not-so-humorous part, to which I've already alluded, is that over the course of human history—particularly in the West—people have been persecuted, tortured, and even put to death over lesser or finer points of theology and belief than what is contained in this fanciful and comedic routine. And the means of execution, quite often, was far worse than getting tossed off a bridge.

I only need to go to the history of my own faith tradition for an example. On October 27, 1553, Michael Servetus, regarded as the founder of Unitarianism, with his publication of *On the Errors of the Trinity,* was burned at the stake at the behest of one of the leading lights of the Protestant Reformation, John Calvin. It took place in the supposedly enlightened city of Geneva, Switzerland. According to the accounts of his execution, Servetus's last words were "O Jesus, Son of the Eternal God, have mercy upon me." When told of this, Calvin's alleged reply was that if the condemned man had proclaimed Jesus as "the Eternal Son of God" rather than the "Son of the Eternal God," his life would have been spared. That was Servetus's capital crime: he believed Jesus to be the Son of God, but not God Himself (i.e., the *Eternal* Son of God) as the classic Christian doctrine of the Trinity holds. It was Servetus's unwillingness to rearrange his words that cost him his life in a horribly excruciating manner.

For all the laughs I get from Mr. Philips comedic bit, when I place it in this kind of a broad historical context, it becomes a little less funny.

The title of this chapter is "Belief *versus* the Religious Impulse" for reasons I've already touched on. Another of my colleagues in the Unitarian Universalist ministry, the Reverend Peter Morales, takes it a step further when he calls belief the *enemy* of religion. In an essay for one of our denominational publications, Peter wrote,

> We are so immersed in a culture that views religion as a matter of what people believe that we think this is the way it has always been. It isn't. All of this emphasis upon what someone believes is actually very modern and very Western. . . . Buddhism has no theology in the way we use the word (and) doesn't even have a God in the usual sense.

Peter continues,

> Jews never had anything like a creed, a statement of belief. Ironically, Jesus, about whom there are all sorts of creeds, probably never encountered a creed in his life. . . . Jews did have a definite sense of God. . . . The Hebrew scriptures never show

> an interest in what people believe. [Rather they] show an interest in what people do. They are supposed to love God and obey the commandments. . . . The great [Hebrew] prophets . . . were concerned with justice and compassion. . . . They had no interest in doctrine.

It was not until the rise of the church in the Western world that such a heavy emphasis upon belief as the central factor in religion arose. That was when belief became equated with adherence to a creed or to specifically delineated points of doctrine. And with this came the idea that to be a "believer" in good standing meant taking on that kind of adherence. As just indicated by the Calvin/Servetus episode, the insistence on "correct beliefs" as a way of being properly religious carried right over into the Protestant Reformation, some of whose leaders were quite willing to burn "their heretics" at the stake as well. The Protestant Reformation primarily arose over resistance to some of the more abhorrent practices and excesses of the sixteenth-century Catholic Church than it did over points of doctrine. And whatever points of doctrine were at issue, the outcome was to simply change the insistence upon the "truth" of one set of beliefs for yet another. The true essence of religion got lost in the shuffle.

What then is this "true essence of religion"? I've already offered how Reverends Church and Helverson have answered the question. I'll take another swing at it using a Latin exercise I had to do back in a high school Latin class under the tutelage of one Mrs. Zyler (rest her soul). Anyone who has ever taken a beginning Latin class knows how it goes—you take a multisyllabled English word, break it out into its component parts, find the Latin derivation of each syllable, and then put the English word back together to see what kinds of new understandings of the word you may discover.

Here's what you get when you do that exercise with the word "religion": You get *re* that means "again" as in re-turn. *Ligion* comes from the Latin verb *ligare*, which means "to bind together." It is the same term from which we get our word *ligament*. A ligament is what holds or binds your bones together so that they work in the way they are supposed to. My wife had to have one of her wrists fused because the ligaments in it had deteriorated to the point that the bones in her wrist would not stay in place, thereby causing a lot of pain.

If we put those two Latin fragments together when it comes to the word *religion*, we get "to bind together again." Religion then, in the most basic sense of the word, is the search for what ultimately binds our lives together, gives them their sense of wholeness, and sustains us again and again over the course of our lives. Religion, in this sense, is a verb. It is an ongoing process in which we engage as we seek greater levels of meaning and wholeness in our lives. This process can involve times of incredible uplift and insight and joy, and it can also flow through some of our soul's deepest and darkest nights. Whether one ever becomes a member of a religious community or not, the process is unavoidable.

Indeed, our beliefs play a role in this process; the crucial question is "What kind of belief, and what kind of role?" They can be stepping stones or ports of call in a greater and ongoing journey. Or they can short-circuit the journey if one feels that any single port of call contains the whole truth or represents the final destination.

My beliefs have markedly changed over the course of my life from the time of that Latin class to which I just referred. But however much they have changed—however much I have moved from one stepping stone to the next—they have all served the same impulse, namely, my search for what continues to bind my life together. Call it what you will—especially if the word "religion" is a stumbling block for you—but in one way or another, this drive toward some binding principle in your life will always be there.

I'll make one more pass at Reverend Morales on this matter of belief. In the same essay as cited, he also writes, "The whole idea of belief has gotten twisted. . . . 'Belief' once meant 'what I give my heart to' or 'what I commit myself to.' [It] did not mean agreeing with a set of metaphysical or theological propositions." Peter says this notion of belief "once meant;" I say it still does. Any affirmations we come to as we move through our ports of call are ones in which we are called to examine what it is we give our hearts to and what our ultimate commitments are.

In the chapters that follow, I'll hone in a little more closely on what some of my stepping stones have been when it comes to my understanding of things such as thanksgiving and gratitude, grace, miracles, faith, the holy, and the problem of evil. These are some of the topics I have come back to time and again during my career in the ministry. They have been the theme of sermons I have prepared and delivered as well as the subjects of some of the deepest conversations I've had with the people with whom I've shared my ministries.

About those three years I referred to as the time between leaving the Protestant campus ministry and arriving at the Unitarian Universalist Church in Maine: I left Stevens Point for the University of Wisconsin campus in Madison to enroll in a Masters of Social Work program there. I got two takeaways from that: my tremendous respect for social workers and the realization that I couldn't leave the ministry. Two wonderful and gracious people at the First Unitarian Society of Madison, Wisconsin, the Reverends Max Gaebler and Gertrude Lindener took me under their wings and helped me through the process of my becoming a Unitarian Universalist minister.

I moved to Madison with the woman to whom I've now been married for over forty years. We've since been blessed with a terrific son and daughter-in-law and two of the greatest grandchildren on earth!

From Madison, my new wife and I briefly lived in Urbana, Illinois, where I was a part-time staff member of the Unitarian Universalist (UU) Church of Champaign-Urbana, running the church's campus ministry program. While there, I completed the process of becoming a UU minister with the help and guidance of the minister of the Urbana UU Church, the late Rev. Ed Harris. Shortly thereafter, it was on to Rockland, Maine.

Through it all and in all the years since then, I've been blessed with the sustaining friendship of three guys with whom I linked up in the seminary where we forged a bond that has remained in place throughout our lives. With each of us in our seventies now, we make it a point to gather once a year to check in on our lives and to renew our close companionship of over fifty years.

I was especially grateful for their support during the particular time of testing referred to in this chapter. Thanks, Dave, Sam, and Gordon, for your support then and in all the years that have followed. It is to these guys that this book is dedicated.

Chapter 3

WHOM DO WE THANK?

I still get a chuckle every time I recall this incident from the time of my ministry with the First Universalist Church (Unitarian Universalist) of Rockland, Maine, in the early 1980s. I would, from time to time, have an occasion to go over to Augusta, the state capitol, which is about forty miles inland from coastal Rockland. On one of those trips, I stopped by the Augusta Unitarian Universalist Church to visit with a friend and colleague who was the minister there at the time.

As I left the church and crossed the street to where my car was parked, I noticed a woman about a half a block away, walking toward me. As she got closer, I recognized her as someone with whom I served on the board of directors of the local community mental health center in the Mid-Coast Maine region. Her name was Connie. I decided to wait until she got to where I was standing so we could have a chitchat.

As she got closer, I noticed she had a dazed and glazed look on her face to the point that she wasn't even aware of my presence. When she finally got about ten feet away and was still not showing any sign of recognizing me or of even knowing I was there, I said, "Hey, Connie, what's up?"

My words had the effect of snapping her out of a trance. She stared at me with very wide eyes and practically yelled out, "Steve, what are you doing here!"

I was so startled, I actually began to explain, "Well, you see, I was just talking with this minister friend of mine at that church over there, and now I'm getting ready to go back to Rockland." We quickly realized how ridiculous we both sounded and laughed a bit as Connie told me her story.

She was a very active lay leader in her local Episcopal church in Camden, Maine—a tony little town about ten miles up the coast from Rockland. She'd come over to Augusta for a meeting of a committee she served on for her Episcopal diocese. As she was leaving town, her car conked out. She had it towed to the local dealership and service shop for the make of the car, only to be told that it needed a part that would take at least a day for them to get and they had no loaners available. Her husband was out of town on a business trip, and the calls she'd made in an attempt to reach anyone else in Camden who might have come over to her rescue went unanswered. This was back in the Neanderthal age, also known as the pre–cell phone and pre-internet era, so a cell-phone call or a Facebook appeal were not options. In addition, the last bus for the day from Augusta that went over to the coast had already departed.

Feeling completely at loose ends, poor Connie just started wandering down the nearest street in something of a fog about what to do next when she almost quite literally walked right into me. Since I didn't fully pick up on the level of desperation she was feeling, my reaction was pretty nonchalant. I said, more or less offhandedly, "Well, hop in. I'll drive you over to Camden on my way home."

Her eyes got even wider than when she'd first seen me. "You can drive me home?" Staying in a nonchalant mode, I answered, "Sure, we don't live that far apart. Be glad to take you over. Let's go."

Not quite believing what was happening to her, she got in the car and we headed out of town. In a matter of just a few short minutes my friend had gone from feeling completely high and dry and stranded some forty miles from her home to being in a car that would take her right to her front door. For the first several minutes of our trip, she sat in a contemplative silence, processing all that had just happened to her before blurting out, "Steve, now I know it's true. There really is a God!"

I laughed so hard, I nearly drove off the road, which would have certainly taken the edge off the good fortune we were experiencing. When I got over my laughing fit, I said, "Connie, this is really too rich. You're a faithful devoted Episcopalian, and it takes a chance meet-up with a Unitarian Universalist minister to finally convince you of the existence of God!" We were both able to appreciate the humor and the irony in that, and less than an hour later I dropped her off in front of her house in Camden and headed down the coast to my home in Rockland.

I viewed the whole episode as a very fortunate coincidence for Connie. I just happened to be in the right place at the right time for her. The fact of the matter is that had I come out of that church five minutes earlier or five minutes later than I did, the two of us would have never met, and all I've described here never would have taken place.

I know that Connie, resourceful person that she was, would have eventually figured out some way to get herself home. I just happened to catch her when she'd been momentarily knocked out of kilter and was trying to get her bearings. I'm sure as well that part of her exclamation that "There is a God" was an expression of relief and joy and thankfulness that she'd been bailed out of a tough and unexpected situation by doing nothing more than wandering in a fog down a city street.

But in addition to being profusely grateful to me—almost to the point of embarrassment on my part—Connie also felt the need to acknowledge the workings of some greater being or power and to be thankful on that level as well. She needed to offer a "cosmic thank you" so to speak. What I took—and still take—as a purely coincidental meet-up was an indication for her of a greater hand at work; in this case, the hand of God. This hand gave her an unexpected gift and blessing, even if it was delivered by a Unitarian Universalist minister for whom the idea of a Supreme Being doesn't quite work.

There is no point in getting into which one of us was "right." We each had our own interpretations of the same event. And while we each had our differing interpretations, I am like Connie in the sense that I, too, feel a need to offer my own kind of cosmic "thank you" from time to time. I have my moments when life feels especially full for me and when I simply need to say "thank you" for the life I have. Who or what I'm saying "thank you" to doesn't much matter to me. I prefer instead to allow myself to feel blessed by a cloud of mystery, a cloud of wonder, and sometimes a cloud of awe over which I have little, if any, control. But it is a cloud of mystery whose presence I feel nonetheless.

When I get in this frame of mind, I find myself drawn to some very wise words by the late Rev. Raymond Baughn: "Giving thanks has nothing to do with who or what produced the gift. It is rather a way of perceiving our life. Even in the midst of hurt and disappointment, when we see ourselves in a universe that gives us life and touches us with love, we praise."

That sure works for me; thank you, Raymond. My prayer of thanksgiving is not one directed to a deity, but rather it is my way of perceiving life—even when life hurts, wounds, disappoints, frustrates, or angers me. Such a prayer is more of an attempt to cultivate an ongoing attitude of gratitude than of words addressed to a Supreme Being. Such thankfulness, again, is a way of perceiving life and a way of seeing ourselves in a universe that gives us life and in which we find love and care and inspiration. It is cultivating this kind of awareness—that, being human, is an awareness I fall in and out of—that constitutes my cosmic "thank you."

To Ray Baughn's words, I would add those of the fourteenth-century German mystic and theologian Meister Eckhart: "If the only prayer you ever say in your whole life is 'thank you,' that would suffice." Indeed, that *would* suffice. Father Eckhart was a Dominican priest who had to endure several charges of heresy over the course of his life for maintaining that one could experience the divine directly without intercessors, such as the medieval church.

The fact that the church of his day considered such an idea a heresy most likely meant that Father Eckhart was speaking the truth. He was one of those people of faith—men and women who arise over the ages—and who can see beyond the particularities of their own faith to certain larger and universal truths.

"If the only prayer you say in your life is 'thank you,' that would suffice." Like Ray Baughn, Eckhart is speaking more about an attitude or stance toward living than the content of what a prayer of thanksgiving "should" contain or to whom it might be addressed. To simply and profoundly encounter those special moments of blessing in our lives is to offer Eckhart's prayer of thanksgiving, even (or especially) if no words are spoken or no deity is addressed.

While we're on the subject of medieval Catholic mystics with a strong heretical streak, I should also hold up Julian of Norwich. She lived in England about a century prior to Eckhart's time in Germany.

Julian lived a hermitlike, contemplative life within the church at Norwich. She wrote what is believed to be the first book written by a woman in the English language titled *Sixteen Revelations of Divine Love.* In it she held that God was the source and embodiment of universal love and that there was no hell. Julian also believed that God was really a divine She—not He—and compared Jesus Christ to a wise, merciful, and loving mother. Like Eckhart, she too saw beyond the bounds of her own faith to its universal implications and meanings.

Julian, or Juliana as she was sometimes called, and Meister Eckhart were both prolific writers by the standards of their day, and like Eckhart, Julian of Norwich has one particular line for which she is especially noted and remembered. She said it came to her from God in one of her mystical visions, in which She (that is to say, God) said to her (that is to say, Julian), "All shall be well, and all shall be well, and all manner of things shall be well."

Julian lived in England during one of the more virulent outbreaks of the Black Plague. People by the scores really and truly dropped like flies. In the cities, there was a crisis about what to do with the bodies since they couldn't all be properly buried. The corpses had to be carted off en masse and dumped in large pits on the outside of the towns.

However cloistered she may have been, Julian had to know about the Black Plague. It might have seemed blasphemous in that kind of setting to speak the words "All shall be well, and all shall be well, and all manner of things shall be well" and attribute them to a loving and maternal God.

And yet these simple words have endured over the centuries, even finding their way into the poetry of T. S. Eliot.

Like Eckhart's, these words also strike a universal chord. As I read them and ponder over them, I hardly think Julian was saying that everything is always hunky-dory. All she had to do was look around her, as she surely must have done, to know that wasn't the case. What I take from these words as I read them through my religious humanist lens is the affirmation that Life and Love, with capital *Ls*, are ultimately stronger and more resilient than death and despair and hatred—however much these latter things may seem to hold sway at any given time.

Julian's words are also a call to those who hear them and who truly get their message to hold fast to what is good, to practice kindness, and to stand on the side of love.

"All shall be well, and all shall be well, and all manner of things shall be well."

"If the only prayer you say in your life is 'thank you,' that would suffice."

I would offer that these words of Julian and Eckhart constitute prayers anyone can say whenever their circumstances call for it and whatever "God" may or may not mean to the one praying.

I have one more round to go with Ray Baughn. He writes of being thankful "even in the midst of hurt and disappointment." Hurt and disappointment and the pain of loss are realities we come up against as much, if not more, regularly than our "thank you" moments. We experience our lives in the push and pull between Eckhart's "thank you" and Julian's "all shall be well" on the one hand, and all those things that diminish and demean and cheapen life on the other. Such is the inescapable tension in which we have to live.

It is in that tension that there are some certain and simple truths I find worth holding on to. I'll state them personally while knowing—and hoping—they reach beyond me.

However it may have been given to me, I'm living the only life I have during the only time given me to live it and on the only earth and in the only universe I have in which to live it. What other choice do I—do we—have but to accept these truths and live with them and say yes to them? We are aware of the unfinished and unhealed parts of the world where we live, just as we're aware of the unfinished and unhealed parts of our own lives. But we must still give thanks. If ours were not a life and if ours were not a world for which we can give thanks, then why would we even care about our lives or our world in the first place?

To say "thank you" or "all shall be well", then, is not to approve of all that comes your way or that gets visited upon you. Rather it is to face and take all that life gives us and then using the will, the resources, and the power of the human spirit, we can become agents of transformation. We become agents of transformation for ourselves, for those with whom we are in community, and for a world that stands in need of our care, our love, and our commitment.

At an earlier place in this chapter, I noted, "To simply and profoundly encounter those special moments of blessing in our lives is to offer Eckhart's prayer of thanksgiving, even (or especially) if no words are spoken." In writing this line, I recalled a passage in an essay by the late novelist Kurt Vonnegut. Vonnegut was an avowed atheist who still could not fully and finally let go of the idea of God.

In an interview he gave for the British *Weekly Guardian* as recounted in his book *Fates Worse than Death,* Vonnegut recalls being asked, "What is your idea of perfect happiness?" He answered, "Imagining that something somewhere wants us to like it here." *Imagining,* please note, that "something somewhere wants us to like it here."

Later in that same interview, he is asked, "When and where were you most happy?" With a brief story, he answered, "[Years ago], my Finnish publisher took me to a little inn on the edge of the permafrost in his country. We took a walk and found frozen ripe blueberries on bushes. We thawed them out in our mouths. It was as though something somewhere wanted us to like it here."

That was an eternal moment of thanksgiving for Vonnegut. For all the success and fame and wealth that in time came his way, his life knew more than its share of tragedy. He was raised in a family where his mother was subject to fits of screaming madness. He was an American soldier in a World War II prisoner-of-war (POW) camp in Dresden, Germany, when allied forces bombed that purely civilian city. And he had to help with gathering up the dead bodies in its aftermath. His son suffered a schizophrenic breakdown. His first wife died of cancer. He came very close to suicide in one of his several battles with depression.

Maybe what sustained him was his cultivating of the idea that "something somewhere wants us to like it here." Note again his use of the word "imagining." Imagining is not the same thing as believing in. Imagining, as I feel Vonnegut used the term here, means "holding out for the possibility." That was the best he could do, and for Kurt Vonnegut, that sufficed.

Some years after reading this account, I had my own "blueberries on the permafrost" moment. It was in a quite different part of the world with a very different climate than that of Finland—California's Big Sur Country.

I'd spent the night sleeping in a recreational vehicle (RV) with a couple of friends on the grounds of a really funky place called the Henry Miller Memorial Library. It's a combination bookstore, outdoor performing arts center, and literary hangout not far from where the novelist and essayist Henry Miller lived during the Big Sur phase of his life. My buddies and I were on for a program there the following day.

I woke up just before daybreak, needing to answer the call of nature most of us experience upon waking. I quietly got dressed, slipped out the door, and made my way over to a restroom. As I started back to the RV, I decided not to risk waking up the two guys who were still sleeping. Instead, I opted for a walk along California's Route 1 highway.

As the old Easter hymn has it: "My Lord, what a morning!" The Miller Library sits at the bottom of a small valley, so my walk along Route 1 took me up a winding hill alongside the highway. The summer traffic had not yet started. The sky was becoming increasingly clear. The Pacific Ocean to my left was as blue as an ocean can get and seemingly went on forever. On my right, the early morning sunlight was just starting to make its way through a redwood forest. There was a thin and slowly disappearing layer of fog right at the tops of the trees.

About halfway up the hill, I stopped dead in my tracks. I could not take another step. There it was. I was standing right in the midst of the signature song of one of my American heroes, Woody Guthrie: "California . . . walking that ribbon of highway . . . redwood forest . . . sun shining . . . fog lifting . . ." It was right there. I couldn't move. I noticed I was standing next to a log, so I managed to sit and let the moment have its way with me. While sitting in silence, on some barely conscious level of my being, I offered Eckhart's "thank you."

Even eternal moments don't last forever. A delivery truck went by on its way to the nearby Nepenthe Restaurant. That was enough to break the spell. As I walked back down the hill to join my friends, I felt a connection with Vonnegut in that I, too, had now had my experience of *imagining* that something somewhere wanted me to like it here.

And that was sufficient.

Chapter 4:

Fake It Till You Make It or Living by Faith

Near the end of my seminary years, I discovered the writings of Jack Kerouac. I knew he was the author of *On the Road* but didn't really start to explore his writings until after he died in 1969. By then he was largely considered a literary has-been who had died the tragic death of an alcoholic. Several of his novels were out of print. I was especially taken with *The Dharma Bums* that had stayed in publication and described the affinity he developed for Buddhism while remaining a lifelong Catholic. I found I liked Kerouac's writing style and proceeded to read whatever of his works were available. Five of his novels are based on his growing-up days in Lowell, Massachusetts, and I was actually more impressed with them than by his "road" novels.

Then in the summer of 1988, I became the minister of the Unitarian Universalist Church of Nashua, New Hampshire. Nashua is about fifteen miles north of Lowell. By now a Kerouac Renaissance was underway. Many of his works were being brought back into print, along with those being posthumously published, as his true literary talents were coming to be widely recognized and appreciated. Part of that renaissance included an annual Kerouac festival being put on in his hometown of Lowell.

A few years after getting settled in my Nashua ministry, I decided to check out the committee down in Lowell that produced the Kerouac festivals. I got myself invited to one of their meetings, and while I thought they were a good group of people with whom I shared some literary interests, I wasn't so sure I wanted to get caught up in the nuts and bolts of producing a festival every year. I mostly dabbled around the edges of the committee—known as Lowell Celebrates Kerouac—without making any strong commitments. I knew my knowledge of the author's life and work was fairly good but still not as much as some of the other committee members.

Then as the time for the 1993 festival approached, I got a call from one of the committee members. Would I chair a panel symposium during the festival weekend on "Kerouac and Spirituality"? Since I'd been a no-show at most of the planning meetings in the prior months, I was surprised to be asked. But maybe they figured, what with me being a minister and all, that I was supposed to know something about the subject. So I said okay, I'll do it.

It wasn't until a week or so later that I thought to ask someone on the committee who would be on the panel. Turned out it was a couple of local poets, and, oh yeah, Allen Ginsberg is coming. Whoa, hold on—I'm supposed to *lead* a symposium with Allen Ginsberg on Kerouac's spirituality? I'd always wanted to meet the guy, but to hold my own in a conversation with him in front of what we knew would be a large crowd of people—that was another matter altogether. But rather than admit to all these misgivings and second thoughts, I said, "Hey, that's great."

The day arrived. The meeting room was packed. I'd deliberately dressed down for the occasion. So naturally, Ginsberg showed up clean shaven, well groomed, and in a suit and tie, playing against type of the hairy wild-man poet image he'd cultivated for much of his life. He sat next to me, extended his hand, and said, "Hi, I'm Allen Ginsberg." (Like I hadn't figured that out!)

Feeling a bit overwhelmed already, I looked up and saw one of Kerouac's principal biographers, Dr. Ann Charters, sitting in the front row. She is generally regarded as one of the better-informed historians of the whole "Beat" era, and she and Ginsberg were longtime friends. She had her notepad and pencil all poised. A few seats behind her was a woman who, Allen informed me in a whisper, was Kerouac's girlfriend from around the time in his life that we were going to be discussing.

All I could think was "What am I doing here?" I wondered if there was a back door where I could slip out before anyone figured out that I was an imposter. In order to look like I knew what I was doing, I glanced down at my "prepared remarks" that were supposed to launch the discussion. All that got me was "What a load of hooey this is—you can't say this crap out loud in a room full of people!"

Well, it was about then that I gave myself a metaphorical slap up side of the head, told myself to quit whining to myself, and summoned up a bit of wisdom I've long carried around. "Just fake it till you make it . . . and get this show underway." I figured, okay, I don't quite know what I'm doing here, but I'll act as if I do and see what happens. And somewhere along the way, my feelings of faking it got tamped down at least enough that I began to enjoy mixing it up with all those on the panel, including Mr. Ginsberg.

I still didn't have a particularly good sense of how the whole event had gone, though, until a week or so later when the committee got together for a post-festival evaluation meeting. A lot of the conversation was about how well the symposium had gone—for which I was frequently thanked. I decided I hadn't made a complete fool out of myself after all. I even allowed myself to think that maybe, in addition to my ministry, I might have a future with this whole Kerouac/Beat business.

Some future it turned out to be. A few years later, I was the president of the festival organization and teaching some Beat literature classes at the University of Massachusetts at Lowell. I went on to write a couple of books on Kerouac and some of the other Beat Generation writers. And it all began when somebody asked me to do something I wasn't sure I could do. An episode of major self-doubt proved to be a pivotal life moment for me.

"Fake it till you make it" was the stance or attitude that got me through the experience just described. At first hearing, that phrase may sound as if I were being an advocate for phoniness or pretense, but not really. I use the expression to describe a circumstance where you don't quite know what you're doing but know you have to act anyway, or where you don't know with absolute certainty that the stance you're taking is the right one but still have to take a stand.

In the end, "fake it till you make it" is not about being phony or inauthentic. Instead, it's about trusting yourself while in the midst of uncertain or difficult circumstances as you are trying to get your bearings. It's about cultivating a capacity for self-trust. It's really about living by faith.

Living by faith, in one way of another, is what I've been doing all my life. I've always considered myself a person of faith. It's just that the nature of my faith and the object—make that objects—of my faith have changed over the course of my life in ways I've already indicated.

In thinking of my symposium experience, I recalled something I'd read in a book titled *And a Voice to Sing With.* The book is Joan Baez's autobiography. In it Ms. Baez tells of frequently having feelings before a concert similar to the ones I described as having before that symposium: self-doubt, inadequacy, "what do I think I'm doing here?" kinds of feelings. I was amazed to read that. Ms. Baez has had one of the most clear and beautiful singing voices I've ever heard over several decades now. It's dropped a register or two as she gotten older, but still . . . it's beautiful. Joan Baez's mantra in such preconcert moments of self-doubt, as she tells it in her book, was to say to herself, "Put it in the hands of God," and pick up her guitar and walk out and do her concert.

Reading that got me thinking (and here comes the theological part): When I say, "Fake it till you make it," and Joan Baez says, "Put it in the hands of God," are we—each in our own way—saying the same thing? I can't say for sure, of course. I had the pleasure of briefly meeting this woman many, many years ago, but we didn't talk about God.

"Put it in the hands of God." "Fake it till you make it." Is this a case of a different language being used for similar phenomena? Could they both be similar statements of faith with alternate wording?

One way to flesh out the term *faith* a little more would be to consider what it means to be a person of faith since I've already referred to myself as such. We can come at the matter by looking at two modes of faith. There may be some fancy theological terms we could come up with for each mode, but we'll keep it simple by calling them mode 1 and mode 2. They differ with respect to the realms in which they are ultimately vested or anchored.

At the risk of oversimplification, but to give us a couple of handles to work with, mode 1 is vested in the realm of the supernatural, albeit with *supernatural* being understood in more than one way. Mode 2 faith operates within the workings of the natural world, with the concession that there is still much we do not know about the natural world and universe and their workings.

Both of these modes of faith, with their variations, are lived out in this world and in one's day-to-day comings and goings. People of faith in both of these realms or modes will do pretty much the same things from one day to the next: work at their jobs, go shopping, pursue hobbies, tend to their families, go to baseball games, and the like. But they see their world and their lives through differing lenses.

Mode 1 holds that our lives and the life of the earth and universe are ultimately in the hands of a Supreme Being referred to by a variety of names—God, Jehovah, the Lord, Allah, etc., depending upon the particular religion in which it is set. Quite often the will, intent, and commands of this Supreme Being are revealed through a sacred text—a text, even if not taken literally, that is still accorded the utmost seriousness and authority. It is this kind of God who gives meaning, purpose, and direction to the lives of those in mode 1 faith. And without such a God, there is no final meaning, purpose, or direction to one's life.

This is the nature of the faith in which I was raised, and while it is a mode I no longer embrace, I do not disparage those who do. Such faith is a sustaining force in millions of lives. Richard Dawkins, as we've seen, would call this kind of faith a delusion. Maybe so, but it's a delusion that works pretty well.

Then there's mode 2 faith. This one is solely located within the realm of the natural world and universe, acknowledging, as I just did, that there is still much we do not know about this "realm of the natural world and universe." To be a person of faith in this mode means you trust in the human capacity for reason and in exercising the strength of the human will and spirit.

To be sure, in order to honestly operate in this mode of faith, one also has to acknowledge that trusting in reason and exercising the strength of the human will and spirit only goes so far. You are still left with the need or urge to respond to Helverson's religious impulse. You still find yourself seeking, in Forrest Church's language again, "that which is greater than all and present in all." For me, as a mode 2 guy, "that which is greater than all and present within all" finds expression within the realm of the natural. It is that depth dimension to life that I call sacred or holy and that can be touched and experienced.

People in both of these modes of faith can speak of God, but they are speaking of differing realities. In mode 1, as just noted, God is a Supreme Being who exists outside of the natural realm and who rules over the natural world and over our lives as we live in this world. In mode 2, God is more likely seen as what Ralph Waldo Emerson and others called one's divine spark, the god or goddess within, or the blessed spirit of life. This "inner spark" also connects us to all that is beyond us, to what we know, and to what we do not know.

I was in "mode 2 faith" back at that symposium. I decided I've just got to let it go and let it happen, and assume that—by faith—I'd still be on my feet when it's done. Fake it till you make it, that is to say, while believing that you will indeed make it. I don't know for sure that Joan Baez is a "mode 2" person of faith, but if she is, then her phrase "Put it in the hands of God" isn't too different from my own.

Some help in understanding mode 2 faith can also be found in the writings of William James. James was a nineteenth-century philosopher and psychologist and has been deemed the "father of American psychology." He taught the first psych courses to be offered at Harvard University in the late nineteenth century. His brother Henry was a noted American novelist and short-story writer. His wife Alice Gibbons was a prolific nineteenth-century woman of letters. James's father was a noted theologian.

It was due in good measure to the influence of his theologian father that William James developed a strong interest in the role of religion in personal and public life. This interest led him to write his book *The Varieties of Religious Experience.*

In that work, James writes, "It is essential that God be conceived as the deepest power in the universe." I'm not sure about the "essential" part, but James's observation offers a path to mode 2 faith. We are creatures of the universe, along with the stars and planets and galaxies and all the rest. However our earthly lives may have begun, our ultimate origins go back to the Big Bang. If God, to use James's language, is to be regarded as the deepest power in the universe, then does not this same power reside in each of us as creatures of the universe? You need not use Dr. James's terminology to believe that. Since he and Dr. Church lived about a century apart, they obviously never met. But I think Dr. James would have appreciated Forrest's line about God not being God's name but a name for "that which is greater than all and present in all."

To be a person of faith in this Jamesian sense is to trust that you can access the deepest power that is both in you and beyond you. It is to believe that there is a depth to life that you need not go beyond this natural world in order to reach, touch, and experience it. I call it a sacred or holy dimension to life that is available to us if we truly seek and find.

Living a life of faith in this way does not shield one from feelings of doubt and from the experience of betrayal. It offers no protection from being let down or, on occasion, letting others down. This kind of faith is not to be confused with certainty. Instead, it means recognizing that we live in a world and universe that blesses us in some very wonderful and life-fulfilling ways at times and in some inexplicably devastating ways at other times. To be a person of faith is to believe in that "deepest power," as James called it, that allows one to respond to both the blessings and the tragedies of life and keep on going for as long as life is yours to have.

There are some more of James's words that further flesh out this type of faith: "Believe that your life is worth living, and your belief will help create the fact. . . . Act as if what you do makes a difference. It does." To believe that we are capable of living worthy and meaningful lives will, as James puts it, "create the fact." That is living by faith.

I like James's use of the two simple words *as if.* To live a life of faith is to live "as if." My symposium story was my lighthearted and fun way of making that point. I got over my self-doubt by acting "as if" I could do what I was supposed to do and was expected to do. I admit that my "fake it till you make it" line is a frivolous way of making a serious point. For to truly live, "as if" goes way beyond a fun type of story when in it comes to a life of faith.

"Act as if what you do makes a difference. It does." As valuable as it is to heed this message on a personal level, it goes well beyond the personal when it comes to our envisioning the world where we wish to live and wish to leave for those who come after us. We must live as if our justice-seeking efforts for a safer, saner, and more peaceful world will make a difference. We must act as if the forces of bigotry and hatred and ignorance will not have the last word. In this sense, we must live with the deepest faith we can muster and act on it in whatever ways we can.

I go one more round with mode 2 faith by citing yet another of my theological mentors, the theologian and philosopher Sam Keen. He offers a delightful little riff on faith in his well-traveled book *To a Dancing God.* As much as I appreciate the academic tone of Dr. James's writing, I also like Dr. Keen's take on faith by his use of a cartoon:

> Sylvester the cat is running away from his ancient enemy the bull dog. Suddenly he sees that the only way of escape open to him is across a pond. Without hesitating he runs out onto the water with no worry about sinking. So long as he remains un-anxious, a lily pad arises to meet each of his advancing feet a split second before he would otherwise sink into the water. Suddenly, he becomes alarmed, for although his feet have found support for his journey thus far he can see no visible means of support for the remainder of the trip across the pond. The moment he begins to worry whether

> or not the next lily pad will appear on schedule, he sinks into the water and the bulldog stands on the shore and laughs.

Playing off this image, Keen continues,

> When I cease asking for guarantees that my feet will find secure ground, support appears for my advancing steps. *The trick is to stop demanding certainty and trust in the ability of the self to respond creatively to whatever happens* [emphasis added].

At a later point in this same chapter, Keen calls the stance he's describing "trustful agnosticism." That designation works for me. One of the great blessings of my life is that those lily pads, in one form or another, have arisen to meet my steps, however faltering they may have been at times and however uncertain the way across the pond may have been on occasion. I've found I do not need to fully know what the ultimate source of those lily pads may be in order to keep trusting in their presence: trustful agnosticism.

One of my books that came out in 2007 recounts the life and ministry of a wonderful poet, friend, and colleague the late Rev. Ric Masten. As Ric faced the final stage of his life while battling prostate cancer, one of his "cancer poems" as he called them, had this line:

It's only in uncertainty that true hope can be found,

And you can bet a sure thing will always let you down.

It was when Ric let go of any need for certainty about how and when his life would end that he found he could live in hope and creativity for all that remained of his life. Paradoxical as it may sound, I call that living by faith.

Our faith journeys are ones that go forth within this precious, fragile, sacred, and time-bound life for as long as we are given to live it. My faith stance is that the journey is worth the making and the taking for the sake of the journey itself and that life is worthy of waking up to and realizing.

As for a final destination, I put that in the hands of, well, "God."

Chapter 5

WHAT OF MIRACLES?

Another strand of my religious and spiritual travels that I'm weaving into these pages has to do with the death of my father. He was only sixty-nine years old when he passed away. His name was Gordon, and he grew up in the back country of rural West Virginia as he came of age in the 1920s. He moved to that state's capitol of Charleston in the midst of the Depression to find work and developed a skill for house painting. His formal education went to the eighth grade.

Gordon Edington returned to Charleston and to his house painting after his service in the Navy in World War II, with a British-war bride and a newborn son (yours truly). It was there that he and his wife, my mother, raised their family that came to include my three younger sisters. It was a struggle for my parents. Money was often tight. Even as a youngster, I was aware how hard my dad worked just to keep us housed, fed, and clothed.

My father's faith in God, as worshipped in the evangelical Baptist church to which he brought his family, was what sustained him. He was a Deacon. Five or six days a week, he wore work clothes that smelled of paint. On Sunday, he wore a suit and was Mr. Edington, Church Deacon.

When my wife and I got married in the summer of 1978, things had taken a good turn for my mom and dad. They had found a measure of financial stability. My sisters and I were all married and on with our lives. It was time for my parents to get back some of what they'd sacrificed on our behalf. It was their time now.

It didn't work out that way. In the fall of that same year of 1978, my father began having what was initially diagnosed as a series of small strokes that slightly hampered his ability to walk but did not appear to be all that serious. What was really going on, as a CAT scan eventually revealed, was a rapidly growing brain tumor. An operation to have it removed was only partially successful, and my father died in late January of 1979 when he had a heart attack on his way home from the hospital a few days after his surgery.

While it was never fully determined, it is quite likely that the tumor—which was a very rare type—was caused by the fumes my father inhaled from the lead-based and oil-based paint he used for many years before water-based, or latex, paint came into widespread use. In a way analogous to black lung disease, which is far from unknown in that part of West Virginia, my father's death was, in good likelihood, caused by his work.

It all seemed so unfair to me. My dad had gotten to where he could finally live a more relaxed life, and he died of a brain tumor that was probably caused by all the work he had done for so much of his life. I was just coming into the Unitarian Universalist ministry when this happened. For all the grief I felt over the loss of my father and for all my righteous anger over his not getting the life I felt he deserved for all the work he'd done, I felt there was no One—with a capital *O*—for me to be mad at. Unlike Tevye in *Fiddler on the Roof*, I could not and did not shake my fist at God. My grief and my anger were mine to deal with.

I would think on my father's death from time to time as my life moved along. His passing particularly came back to me some years later when *Time Magazine* ran a cover story with the title "Can We Still Believe in Miracles?" Since it was the pre-Easter issue, the hook had to do with how believable or not the New Testament accounts of the bodily resurrection of Jesus are today. The authors rounded up the usual suspects of conservative to liberal theologians to weigh in.

It was all predictable. The conservatives insisted on a literal interpretation not only of the resurrection accounts but also of all the miracles attributed to Jesus, if the Christian faith was to have any validity at all. The liberals, again quite predictably, said that the accounts of the resurrection and of the miracles Jesus performed can be read on a more metaphorical or symbolic level having to do with his bringing new life, new hope, and new healing to the people he encountered. It was probably interesting to many of *Time Magazine*'s readers, but having been in such conversations numerous times myself by then, I found the article pretty ho-hum.

But what brought back the memories of my father's death was a side story that did a much better job of grabbing my attention than the dueling theologians did. It was about a young girl named Elizabeth Jernigan. Very early on in her childhood, her parents noticed that she had a droopy eyelid. Her grandfather, who was a Harvard trained surgeon, urged the parents to take their daughter to a neurologist. The neurologist discovered a brain tumor. An operation followed in which the part of the tumor that was causing the droopy eyelid was removed. This cost Elizabeth the use of that eye. But the tumor itself was discovered to be malignant and progressive to the point of being eventually fatal.

Elizabeth's parents, as I'm sure you can imagine, were devastated. What parents wouldn't be? Their religion was mainline Episcopalian, which is far from being a faith-healing cult that substitutes God for medical intervention. Still, the Jernigans and their friends prayed for Elizabeth's recovery against seemingly impossible odds. Their priest anointed Elizabeth with oil especially consecrated—according to the dictates of their faith—for the purpose of healing.

A second operation was scheduled to alleviate some of the young girl's pain by removing the fluid around the tumor, but there was no expectation of any recovery beyond that. A few hours before the operation was to take place, however, very little fluid could be detected, and the operation was suspended. The fluid ceased to accumulate. Even more amazing, the tumor itself eventually disappeared. A CAT scan couldn't find a thing.

The sidebar article concluded with these words from Elizabeth's father: "If you happen to see a young girl walking down the street with her eye permanently closed, please do not think some tragedy has befallen her . . . Instead, have cheerful thoughts . . . knowing that our God is powerful, benevolent, and magnificent." In looking for an update on this amazing story, I did a Facebook search for Elizabeth Jernigan and found an account of her wedding. A happy ending indeed.

This was, needless to say, a very powerful and moving and joyful story. I still wonder what to make of it. If a team of neurosurgeons and physicians could not explain the disappearance of a supposedly malignant tumor, I know I can't. The Jernigans, as noted, were hardly devotees of the kind of faith healing that shuns medical intervention. They placed their daughter in the best medical hands they could find and then prayed for a miracle, which, as far as they were concerned, is just what they got.

I certainly have no desire to demean or diminish Mr. Jernigan's faith in a powerful, benevolent, and magnificent God who—as he saw and believed—caused his daughter's tumor to go away. I could not, in Mr. Jernigan's eyes, do that even if I wanted to. I do not belittle the religious faith of the Jernigans and others like them who have experienced similar apparently "miraculous" events.

I have another perspective, another way of looking at things, however, within which I try to place a story like this one. In framing that perspective, I cannot help but think on the way in which my father died and that young Elizabeth Jernigan lived. I am not, at this point in my life, bitter or angry over my father's death. I have plenty enough distance on it by now to know that his brain was invaded by a rare kind of tumor that took his life. The tumor, of course, had no will of its own. It did what tumors usually do, and my father died as a result. It was a painful and tragic loss for me and my family. We relied on the love and support we found with one another and, in time, moved on with our lives.

All that said, when I came across the Jernigan story, heartwarming as I found it to be, I could not help but wonder, *What about the tumor my dad had?* He was one of the most devoutly religious people I've known. He believed in a powerful, benevolent, and magnificent God as deeply as the Jernigans did. But his tumor didn't disappear, and he and my mother did not get the "golden years" they more than deserved. Furthermore, the members of my father's Baptist church prayed just as fervently for his recovery as the members of the Jernigan's congregation prayed for Elizabeth's recovery.

To reiterate, I do not offer these thoughts out of any kind of bitterness or cynicism. I offer them instead as a cautionary tale when it comes to our determining what constitutes a miracle and to what or whom we attribute its workings. I have not stricken the word *miracle* from my vocabulary. I believe it has its appropriate and meaningful uses and understandings. We'll get to them as we go along here.

To give us a working handle, let's consider the differing ways in which a miracle, so named, is viewed. One view is that of a Supreme Being who can and does intervene on occasion in the workings of the natural world to gain an intended outcome. This is a God, if the New Testament Gospels are taken literally, who can cause a dead body to come back to life, make blind people see, or alter the chemical content of water so that it becomes wine. To bring it more up to date, it is also a God who can cause a malignant tumor to disappear.

Another view, call it the naturalist position, is that no event takes place outside the workings of the laws of nature, however "miraculous" it may seem to human beings at any point in human history. What may seem to be the act of an intentional Supreme Being is really a natural event whose cause has not yet been discovered or revealed.

Our early human ancestors, for example, believed eclipses of the sun or moon were caused by the gods or goddesses they worshipped and, as such, were regarded as miracles. They were taken as a sign from their gods and goddesses as either a good or evil omen, depending upon who was interpreting the meaning of the miracle. They knew nothing of the rotations of the earth and the moon and how, at certain times, those rotations and movements cause eclipses. Within the framework of what was known and unknown at that time, their beliefs were not irrational.

Your naturalistic theology types—like, say, me—hold that creation is of one piece, and all that takes place does so within the workings of what the natural world naturally does. And granted, sometimes these workings are beyond our ability to understand them, given the context of what we know at any given point in human history. Such was the case with Elizabeth's tumor. No naturalistic explanation was available, so the vanquished tumor was attributed to the workings of a powerful, benevolent, and magnificent God. It's a perfectly understandable response.

But to play this out a bit further, for all the fantastic insights medical science has given us about the workings of the human body, the human brain remains the body organ about which we know the least. We seem to have the workings of the heart, liver, lungs, etc., down pretty well. But even with all the wonderful discoveries of neuroscience, the workings of the human brain still hold a lot of mystery. Perhaps at some point, neuroscience will uncover why some brain tumors atrophy and disappear on certain rare occasions, while most of the others continue with their deadly growth unless a successful neurosurgery intervenes.

For now, all I can say is that some as yet unknown process took place in the brain of Elizabeth Jernigan that caused her tumor to disappear, and she lived. It was a process that did not take place in the brain of my father, and he died. So it goes. (Thank you, Kurt Vonnegut.)

I wrote earlier that in presenting the cases of both my father and the Jernigans, I was seeking to offer a cautionary tale. It's a tale that calls for some theologizing about the idea, or ideas, of God that come into play as these two cases are considered. As already noted, I do not fault the Jernigans for attributing the recovery of their daughter to the act of a powerful, benevolent, and magnificent God.

Nevertheless, the question I have to raise, however heartwarming we find their story, is "Do we really want to ascribe that kind of power to God?" Once you ascribe to God the power and intent to intervene in the workings of the laws of nature (the laws we've figured out and the ones we've not yet uncovered), you then give that same God the power and the option of withholding His or Her or Its (choose your pronoun) intervention as well. To bring it down to the cases we're looking at, if an all-powerful and intentional God eradicated Elizabeth Jernigan's brain tumor, then I see no other conclusion possible than that this same all-powerful and intentional God allowed the tumor my father had to take his life.

I'm hardly the first to struggle with this conundrum. It's the same one John Calvin and the Calvinists who followed in his stead had to face. Their starting position was that an all-powerful and omnipotent God alone had the power to save souls from the damnation of original sin. If this were the case, then—to be theologically consistent—this same God, so the Calvinists had to acknowledge, also had to have the power to will other souls to eternal damnation. A God with the power to save also had to be a God with the power to damn; otherwise, He (and for those guys it was a "He") was not an all-powerful God. This is what the Calvinists called the doctrine of the elect. The people who attained salvation were those whom an all-powerful god "elected" to save. I'll give the Calvinists credit for consistency while also noting that it is a very cruel consistency.

(Side bar: It was the Unitarians, among others, who countered Calvinist theology by, first, disavowing the idea of original sin and, second, by advocating what they called *salvation by character*. We'll pick this up later in a chapter on salvation.)

When we bring all this back to the cases before us, we run into a similar kind of Calvinist conundrum. Our cases involve brain tumors; they do not have to do with eternal salvation or eternal damnation. But they still raise the same kinds of questions or challenges about what kind of actions we want or think we want when it comes to the workings of a supposedly all-powerful God. Do we really want a God who can intervene in a healing manner in some people but who allows a disease or malady to run its course with others? I am not willing to go with a Calvinist kind of consistency on this one.

It makes more sense for me to look at it this way: We are each given a life and a larger life within which to live it. Sometimes that life blesses us and graces us in inexplicable ways; other times it wounds us and causes us near unbearable pain, also in inexplicable ways. In the midst of both the blessings and the pains, we have to make choices about how we are going to live and the assumptions we are going to live by. And when we encounter those times when we are blessed and graced in ways we cannot fully comprehend or fully explain, we almost instinctively speak of miracles. I know I do. I said a few paragraphs back that I have not stricken the word *miracle* from my vocabulary. How then do I use the term in ways that are meaningful and fulfilling to me?

I take one of my cues from the world of . . . baseball. More specifically, the baseball that was played by the 1969 New York Mets, the team that is still known to this day as the Miracle Mets.

In 1969 the Mets were still a young National League expansion team who had not even had a winning season in the six years of their existence since their founding in 1962. In those six years, their *best* finish was next-to-last in their league's division standings. But in the 1969 season, they came from completely out of nowhere to win both the National League pennant and the World Series. In one "miraculous" season, the loser Mets became the world champion Mets. They accomplished this, of course, by playing under the same rules and under the same conditions as all the other major league baseball teams did.

Fantasy time: let's play a game within a game. Let's say that in that year of 1969, the commissioner of baseball—who, for all intents and purposes, is the God of Baseball—decided to change the rules just for the Mets. They would get four outs per inning instead of the three that all the other teams get, and they would only need a three-ball count to draw a walk instead of the four-ball count all the other teams needed.

To take this fantasy to even greater heights, let's say there was an omnipotent God who favored the Mets. Under the workings of such a God, routine fly balls hit by Mets's batters would be blown out of the park by sudden gusts of wind for home runs, and for-sure home runs by their opponents would be blown back into the ballpark and caught by Mets outfielders for routine outs.

If the Mets had won their championship under these admittedly absurd circumstances, they would not have been the Miracle Mets. They would have been the artificially manipulated Mets, and their world championship would have been meaningless. The miracle was that they won their championship within the bounds and within the rules of the natural world of baseball.

This gets me to an understanding of a miracle I can well appreciate. It is an event or an experience that surprises us (in a good way) or lifts us out of ourselves or gives us a sense of special blessing, precisely because it takes place within the context of our natural life and the world where we live. It's kinda what the Mets fans felt as the 1969 baseball season came to its miraculous end.

We now move from baseball to Ralph Waldo Emerson who most likely never saw a game of baseball in his life, or what passed for baseball in his day. But he made a similar point as I do with the Miracle Mets, albeit in a more rarified terminology. In writing of the transcendentalist concept of miracles, Emerson said the transcendentalist "believes in miracles, in the perpetual openness of the human mind to the new influx of light and power; he (sic) believes in inspiration and ecstasy." Emerson's Harvard-based nineteenth-century language has something of an elitist tone to it, but what he is saying is that miracles occur in our natural world if we can keep our minds and spirits open to receiving them. They are ones that bring us new understandings, that is, "new influx of light," and a heightened confidence in our human abilities, that is, a "new influx of power."

The broader context for Emerson's words is his sharp critique and challenge to the traditional Christian understanding of miracle as related in the New Testament. This is how he put it: "To aim to convert a man by miracles [in the biblical sense] is a profanation of the soul. . . . The word Miracle, as pronounced by Christian churches, gives a false impression; it is Monster. It is not one with the blowing clover and the falling rain."

"The blowing clover and the falling rain." Look at the world around you, with "perpetual openness of the human mind," in order to receive your everyday miracles. This was what Emerson urged. His message continues to resonate well.

Emerson's companion and compatriot from down the road and out in the woods from his home in Concord, Massachusetts, a one Henry David Thoreau, said the same thing in a much more cantankerous way: "People talk about Bible miracles because there is no miracle in their lives. Cease to gnaw that crust. There is ripe fruit over your head."

A bit harsh there, Henry; you could lighten up a little. But his point that "there is ripe fruit over your head" is well taken. About a century and a half after Thoreau penned these words, a similar sentiment was expressed by the Buddhist monk and teacher Thich Nhat Hanh. He echoes Thoreau in a much kinder and gentler way:

> I like to walk along on country paths, rice plants and wild grasses on both sides, putting each foot down in mindfulness, knowing that I walk on a wondrous earth. In such moments existence is a miraculous and mysterious reality. People usually consider walking on water or in thin air a miracle. But I think the real miracle is not to walk on water or in thin air, but to walk on the earth. Every day we are engaged in a miracle we don't even recognize: A blue sky, white clouds, green leaves, the black, curious eyes of a child—our own two eyes. All is miracle.

Here's what it finally comes down to for me: I give thanks for the miracles that have come my way—some of which I had a hand in creating, but with most of them coming to me by sheer grace. I've known the miracle of a four-decade marriage (part of *that* miracle being that I can still tell the tale), the miracle of the birth of our son and of our two granddaughters. I've been blessed to witness the miracle of transformation in many human lives when the people with whom I've shared my ministries—some of them in great despair—see and act on new possibilities and new promises for themselves. I've known my miraculous moments of Emerson's "inspiration and ecstasy." I've experienced the miracle of return from some of my—thankfully few—dark nights of the soul.

Where is God in all this? It's the miracles I've known that tell me that my searching for and my experiencing of "that which is greater than all and present in all" are worthy of my living.

Chapter 6
WHAT MUST I DO TO BE SAVED?

I've already made numerous references to the southern West Virginia Baptist church where I was raised. I carry many vivid memories of it. Among them are the weeklong revival meetings that were held every few years in the spring. They could be very high drama at times. The visiting evangelist would get to the end of his sermon and segue into the "invitation." The invitation was to come forward to the front of the church and be "saved." We'd always sing the same hymn—"Just as I Am, Without One Plea." I can still recite all four verses from memory.

Some evenings we'd sing the song through several times as long as the evangelist and the church's minister were convinced that there were still some lost souls out in the pews who needed to receive Jesus. That is what salvation in this setting meant. You stood before the congregation and acknowledged that God—through Jesus's life and death—had redeemed you from your sins, and henceforth, you would lead as good and clean a life as you could with the help of God and Jesus.

You had no choice about being a sinner; you were born into it. It was called original sin. But there was no Calvinist doctrine of the elect (see chapter 5) with the Baptists. You could be redeemed from your sinful state, as anyone could, by simple acknowledging it and coming forward to confess and receive Jesus as your savior. Then you'd be baptized—usually a few weeks later—and join the church and live in a redeemed state of grace.

Some of those coming forward would weep both over their lost state and at how joyful they were to be delivered from it. After the service others in the congregation would come forward to offer their support. This could get pretty emotional as well with a lot tears and hugging. Let me tell you it was powerful stuff.

As a kid, I would watch all this with a mixture of awe and fascination and with some discomfort as well, wondering how many more rounds of "Just as I Am" we were going to do before we could all go home. But I knew we had to wait so that the folks who needed salvation could get saved.

My own route to salvation was a comparatively sedate one at age eleven. I had a talk at my home with the minister whom I greatly admired about what it meant to "receive Jesus" and was baptized by immersion (all the way under) a few weeks later. That was it, which was fine by me. Even at that young age, my innate reserve was already well in place. I wanted to be saved, of course, and know that I was going to heaven. I just didn't want a big deal made out of it.

I know it's easy to make light of all that now. But I saw some lives markedly change for the better thanks to this kind of salvation. My father never tired of telling me how his own life would have been a mess had he not found Jesus—and he was probably right. It kept him on the straight and narrow and enabled him to raise his family in a secure and loving setting, often in the face of economic hardship.

I should add that this was well before the evangelical movement got politicized to the extent it has become today. In all those revival meetings, as well as in the Sunday services I attended at that church up to my college years, I recall very few, if any, political issues ever addressed at all. The politicization of America's evangelical movement, seen within the context of its overall history in America, is a fairly recent phenomenon that began in the late 1970s. The revivals I describe took place in the mid-1950s and into the early 1960s.

We now do a twenty-year jump to the mid-to-late 1970s. By now I'd already been through some significant life changes as I reached my thirties. As indicated in an earlier chapter, I'd become quite taken with the humanistic psychology movement—Carl Rogers, Fritz Perls, Barry Stevens, etc. This interest led me to spend a couple of summers hanging out in San Francisco and Berkeley, learning and participating in something called gestalt therapy, whose primary architect was Dr. Perls.

Those summers conjure up another set of vivid memories, such as this one consisting of fifteen people or so sitting in a circle on the floor of a thickly carpeted room with a lot of pillows scattered around. The place is called the Gestalt Institute of San Francisco. It is a long way, in more ways than one, from that Baptist church in southern West Virginia.

In this setting, somebody would take the "hot seat" as it was called. Actually, it just meant sitting in the center of the circle. With the guidance of the group facilitator, they would talk about the things in their life they wanted to change and what was blocking them from doing so. Often painful events would be recalled; greater desires for self-acceptance and personal peace would be voiced. Oftentimes it got pretty emotional, and after some measure of catharsis had been achieved, other group members would move in to offer their emotional support and encouragement with some hugs and tears.

Part of me would be into this scene, while another part of me was up on the ceiling looking down and thinking, *Haven't I been here before?* Not "here" here, but here in the sense that I'd seen this same dynamic at work, albeit with radically different language and assumptions of faith. But it was the same dynamic of people facing the broken parts of their lives and reaching for some greater levels of wholeness and healing and meaning. It was revival time again. Maybe I wasn't all that far from that Baptist church after all. I recall, after one such session, taking a long late-night solitary walk up and down some of San Francisco's hilly streets and thinking, *Geez, maybe these humanists I'm cozying up to want to be saved in their own way as well.*

I also discovered that my personal reserve was still well intact. I had no more desire to sob and honk my guts out in a room full of humanistic psychology types than I'd had in a church full of Baptists. My mind has gone through a lot of changes over the course of my life, but my personality has stayed pretty constant. These workshops were quite transformative for me, however. They caused me to look closely at some personal and professional issues I'd been avoiding. They played a major part, as noted in Chapter 2, in my decision to leave the liberal Christian ministry and enter the Unitarian Universalist ministry.

When it came to assessing the similarities between the two scenes I just described, I recalled a very familiar passage from the New Testament Gospel of John. It's the story or legend of a very learned gentleman named Nicodemus paying a call on Jesus in the manner of a seeker approaching a guru. He asks, "Good Master, what must I do to be saved?" In the manner of a guru offering a cryptic, go-figure-it-out-for-yourself type of answer, Jesus replies, "You must be born again."

In the setting where I first heard these words, the evangelist would take off on his interpretation of what "born again" meant, which usually was done in such a narrow and damning and threatening way that a few years later, during my college days, I dismissed that whole passage. It never occurred to me then that what the evangelist was saying about being born again and about being saved bore no resemblance at all to anything Jesus is ever recorded as having said on the subject.

Ironically, it wasn't until I began taking a more humanistic view of life and religion and spirituality that I decided that Nicodemus, whoever he was, was actually asking the right question and that Jesus, whoever he may have been, gave Nicodemus the correct answer. Hold that thought.

For now we move from the New Testament to a more contemporary text: Dr. M. Scott Peck's book *The Road Less Traveled*. Here's Peck:

> We all have a sick self and a healthy self . . . even if we seem to be totally fearful and completely rigid, there is still a part of us, however small, that wants to grow . . . that is willing to do the work and take the risks involved in spiritual evolution. And no matter how seemingly healthy and evolved we [may be], there is still a part of us, however small, that clings to the . . . familiar . . . [and] desiring comfort at any cost and the absence of pain at any price.

Peck continues, "In this one respect we human beings are equal. Within each and every one of us there are two selves, one sick and one healthy—the life urge and the death urge, if you will. Each of us represents the whole of the human race." Peck's use of the term *sick* in this passage is similar to Huston Smith's use of the term *disease*. Like Dr. Smith, Peck is not talking about a physical or emotional ailment but rather of a sense of brokenness or incompleteness in our lives.

What Peck is describing is a humanistic version of salvation. Stripped of a lot of its cumbersome baggage, salvation means moving from, or being delivered from, a less than healthy state to a more healthy and wholistic one. Most religions, including the Judaic and Christian ones, have an account of human beings living in a perfect or unblemished state as part of their story or their mythology—a Garden of Eden, for example—where there is complete oneness among the self and life or creation or God, however understood. This state is also called unbroken immediacy, that is, no self/world division.

Then something happens to rupture that relationship or that immediacy. We get expelled from the garden, that is to say. In the Genesis version, the sole blame for this rupture is dumped on the protowoman for allowing herself to be tempted by Satan in the form of a snake. There's an example of very bad and destructive imagery, in this case the demonization of women, being used to explain a universal human condition.

Be that as it may, the goal of religion is to restore—or attempt to restore—that original self/world relationship. Remember "re-ligare," *to bind together again.*

But where do these stories of perfection or immediacy, followed by a rupture, ultimately come from? Here we turn to Dr. Carl Jung. I'm not a hard and fast Jungian, but I find wisdom in his work. According to Jung and one of his "disciples", the late Dr. Joseph Campbell, our human stories of our Gardens of Eden, which many religions have in one form or another, come from our collective human subconscious memory of being in a state of complete immediacy with our entire universe—which was when we were in the body of our mother.

I've already offered one interpretation back in this book's introduction of what was going on with Adam and Even in the Garden of Eden. Jung offers another: the myth of the expulsion of Adam and Eve from the Garden of Eden, as he had it, ultimately derives from our collective unconscious memory of being expelled from our mother's womb. So feeling some degree of alienation from ourselves and from the world we see and sense around us is really nothing more than a consequence of our being born. And we only get one biological birth. We get a shot at other kinds of rebirth, however, in light of our feelings of separation.

Stripped of all its guilt-inducing overlays, in fact, this is what the term *sin* really means—separation. The evangelists I listened to back at those revivals actually used the same term—separation. The way they used it, however, was to speak of our separation from God because of our sinful ways. The good news is that God has redeemed us from those sinful ways and from our state of separation from Him by way of the death of his son Jesus. You can heal, that is, "rebind," that separation by accepting Jesus Christ as your Lord and Savior. Like I said, it's powerful stuff.

Powerful or not, in time, that whole schematic ceased to float my boat. But still, in my gut, I knew about separation. Separation, in Forrest Church's language again, from "that which is greater than all and present in all." Separation, that is to say, from what gives our lives their ultimate meaning and purpose and value. The religious or spiritual journey, then, is an ongoing attempt to heal that separation. At this point in my life, I've decided that it is a Journey—with a capital *J*—that never comes to a full completion in our lifetimes. But it is still a Journey that, if well pursued, makes the trip worthwhile.

When I encountered the writing of Scott Peck, I then knew what he was talking about. He does not use the term that much, but he, too, writes of separation. In his case, it is the separation from our healthy selves and separation from the life and world with which we want some reconciliation.

We know there are unhealed parts of our lives, and we know we live in a terribly broken world that calls us to be about restoring—or saving—whatever small parts of it we may be able to address. We are born, as noted then, to feel some degree of dissonance between ourselves and our world, even as we yearn to overcome that dissonance. Or as Joni Mitchell puts it, "We've got to get ourselves back to the Garden." The many and varied religions of humankind, with their various beliefs, practices, and prescriptions, are our human attempts to do just that—get ourselves back to the garden.

I said in the previous chapter that the origins of the faith tradition I serve, by way of my ministry within it, began in part as a protest against the doctrine of original sin and the Calvinist idea that our deliverance from it was solely in the hands of a God who could elect to "save" us or not as He chose. My Unitarian and Universalist forbearers did not deny the reality of evil or that human beings are capable of truly evil deeds. Their argument was that evil or sinfulness is not an endemic condition into which we are born when we draw our first breath. How I have come to deal with the reality of evil is the topic for the chapter that follows this one.

The Unitarians' counterargument to Calvinism was what they called *salvation by character*. For them, the life and teachings of Jesus as recorded in the New Testament Gospels served as a moral guide for attaining this salvation by character. And while the UU faith tradition is no longer specifically Christian-focused, this idea of salvation by character remains with us, and I like it. Salvation by character is a very positive expression of human potential and human possibility. It is an affirmation that we carry within us the wellsprings of hope and courage that allow us to reborn any number of times during our time on earth. On this note, I move to what my understanding of salvation has come to be.

First, it means coming to self-acceptance. I don't mean this in a smug or self-satisfied way. But rather I mean having the wherewithal to look at both the healthy and unhealthy parts of ourselves—the sick parts and the healed parts as Scott Peck would have it—and say yes to the whole thing. There is a certain kind of freedom and deliverance in not demanding perfection of oneself and of being able to say, "Yes, there are some parts of me that are not quite whole just yet, and that's okay." This does not mean that you will stay stuck in your brokenness or your sickness. It means that we move in the direction of our healthy selves by first confronting and acknowledging where we are, which is where the journey of growth begins. To make that move and take that journey is to make a journey of rebirth. It's not always an easy one. I agree with the first three words of Peck's *Road Less Traveled*: "Life is difficult."

I would say that the self-affirmation or salvation of which I speak has its best chance of being realized within a supportive and redeeming community, within a community that is committed to affirming the inherent worth and dignity of every person within it. We need such redeeming communities on our religious landscape within which people can find and build upon the strength of character that will enhance and nurture their healthy selves. Sometimes it is hard to believe you have that strength on your own, but a healing community can allow and enable you to find it. It is this conviction that has kept me in the ministry over the course of my life.

A second component of this humanistic salvation, as I'm calling it, is to live with a sense of being part of something and related to something greater than yourself. As you've read from me already, I'm not much interested in debates over the existence or nonexistence of a being or entity called *God*. I find God-language useful in certain circumstances if it helps point us to a heightened sense of relationship with "that which is greater than we know." I have not banished the word *God* from my vocabulary; I just carefully and sparingly use it.

To put it in more personal terms, I feel no need to be in a relationship with a Supreme Being, but I feel the need for Relationship, with a capital *R*, nonetheless. Part of my own sense of my personal health and wholeness is bound up in my feelings of relationship with a larger whole, the whole of life itself, which contains me within it. Having this sense of relationship with the whole of life is another part of what I call *being saved* as a religious humanist. And every time, that relationship is renewed or reaffirmed is a time of rebirth.

The final piece of this type of salvation—somewhat related to the one I just described—is the ability to see the worthiness of even the smallest of our efforts to bring some greater measure of justice, compassion, love, and peace to this precious and fragile world. Heed the wisdom of Mahatma

Gandhi when he said, "Everything you do [to advance the cause of justice and peace] may seem insignificant. But it is important that you do it anyway."

I feel safe in saying that we who are now living will never see everything that's possible when it comes to humanity achieving its full health and potential. Tragically, I'm afraid, we have to bear witness to our human folly as much as our human wholeness. But there is a certain kind of saving grace in knowing and believing that our words and our deeds will leave something positive in our wake well after the measure of our days is taken. To believe that our efforts during our time on earth will, in some way—even some small way, move us closer to a beloved community of humanity itself is to live by faith. Another of my colleagues in the UU ministry, the Reverend Fred Small, puts it this way in his song "Everything Possible": "The only measure of your words and your deeds will be the love you leave behind when you're gone."

Since I'm referencing ministerial colleagues, I'll also cite the Reverend Dan O'Neal who lost his life to cancer at a relatively early age. Shortly before he passed away, he sent out a very moving meditation. Here's just a part of it: "Thanks for this day, a day in my life. Thanks for the stars, the earth. Thanks for death which makes life so precious and so vibrantly alive. Thanks for it all. No exceptions."

I only slightly knew Dan, but well enough to know that he was not one to sentimentalize or romanticize death. He would not want his colleagues to do so either, and I won't. His death, among other things, was an indication of how the workings of the natural world do not always treat us in benign ways. But what Dan offered in this little meditation was an affirmation made in the face of cruelty. To be able to say "Thanks for it all, no exceptions" of one's life is the mark of a saved life and one that has known its many times of rebirth.

However we end up taking leave of our own lives, and for however long they are ours to have, may we be able to say the same thing when they come to an end.

Chapter 7
THE PROBLEM OF EVIL (ADD D FOR DEVIL)

The problem of evil is usually characterized as the age-old conundrum of how to reconcile the presence of evil with the belief in an all-powerful and loving God. How does an all-powerful, omnipotent, and loving God allow for the existence of evil? Theologians from a wide range of faith traditions and beliefs have twisted themselves in knots over that conundrum for as long as there have been theologians twisting themselves into knots. But that's not the problem being considered in this chapter.

My beginning premise is that once you eliminate an all-powerful, omnipotent, willful, and intentional Supreme Being, you are still left with the presence and persistence of evil. Since religious liberals tend to take a generally optimistic view of human nature and human living, they are also left with a conundrum, whether it involves God or not: How do we reconcile our largely positive view of human beings with some the truly horrific things that some human beings do to other human beings or to other sentient beings of any kind?

As ponderous and deeply troubling as this subject is, however, we begin our consideration of it in a more lighthearted way before taking up the much heavier matters.

In 1954, the novelist Douglas Wallop came out with a nifty piece of fiction titled *The Year the Yankees Lost the Pennant.* Its two principal characters are a middle-aged fan of the old Washington Senators (who have long since become the Minnesota Twins) and the devil.

Wallop's book is one of a number of literary variations that draws on the theme of Goethe's tragedy *Faust.* In this early nineteenth-century dramatic version of a much older German legend, Goethe's Faust sells his soul to the devil in exchange for infinite knowledge. In Wallop's novel, the deal made with the devil is for a somewhat less lofty—but still quite noble—goal, namely, an American League pennant and World Championship for the old Washington Senators. This novel provided the basis for the Broadway musical and subsequent movie *Damn Yankees,* which is a pretty common sentiment in the Boston, Massachusetts, area where I live.

The story, brief as I can make it, goes like this: It's a mid-1950s American summer, and by July, the Yankees are already running away with the American League lead. The hapless Washington Senators are already mired in last place. Joe Boyd, a middle-aged real-estate salesman, is a long-suffering Senators fan. After listening to yet another Senators loss on the radio, he takes a walk around the block in his neighborhood where he lives with his wife Meg. He mutters to himself that he'd sell his soul to the devil if his Senators could just get a good long ball hitter who would win them a pennant. Right on cue, the devil shows up in the person of a Mr. Applegate, a con man and all-around shifty guy.

Applegate offers his deal. He'll turn middle-aged couch potato Joe Boyd into a twenty-year-old stud Joe Hardy and endow him with the best baseball skills any human being ever had in exchange for his soul. Boyd, soon to be Hardy, takes the deal but negotiates an escape clause. He can get out of the deal anytime up until 9:00 p.m. on September 25—the last day of the season. This was before there were playoffs. When the regular season ended, the top two teams in each league went straight to the World Series.

The deal goes forward. Joe Boyd becomes Joe Hardy, gets himself onto the Senators, and carries the team up through the standings in pursuit of the Yankees. There are several subplots to the story. We can only skim over the details. They have to do with Joe's true identity becoming an object of media attention and curiosity, his coming under the spell of a seductive Lola, and his longing for his wife Meg who has reported Joe as a missing person. In order to keep Meg in the story line, Joe Hardy rents a room in her house—his old Joe Boyd room—so he can still have contact with her, even though she doesn't know who he really is. Pulling the strings behind all these machinations is our good old boy and good old devil, Mr. Applegate.

The story wouldn't be a story if it didn't all come down to September 25. The Senators and the Yankees are tied for first place with one last regular season game to go. The book and the play or movie have two different endings, each with the same eventual outcome. In both versions, it's a few minutes before 9:00 p.m.; the game is in the ninth inning with the score tied. Joe yells to Applegate sitting in the stands that he wants out of the deal as soon as nine o'clock arrives.

In the play and movie, Joe is at bat with two strikes on him when nine o'clock comes. He becomes Joe Boyd again while standing at the plate but still manages to muster up enough of whatever he has in him to hit the game winning and pennant-winning home run. In the book version, Joe is on third base representing the winning run. From third base, he yells to Applegate who is sitting in a box seat behind third to release him from their bargain. The batter at the plate gets a hit, and precisely at 9:00 p.m., just as Joe Hardy leaves third base, he becomes Joe Boyd. Somehow he still manages to huff and puff his middle-aged body down the third baseline and slide safely home, beating the Yankees and thereby beating the devil.

In the denouement, Joe, now back to being Joe Boyd again, goes home to Meg. Applegate shows up and tries to get him to become Joe Hardy just one more time for the World Series, which would also allow the devil to reclaim his soul. Joe refuses. He chooses to stay with his wife as a middle-aged real-estate guy Joe Boyd, and the power of love conquers the power of evil—as represented by the devil.

Well, it's all good fun. It's also, in this case, a whimsical reminder of what an enduring image the person of the devil is in our society and culture. In this fanciful tale about the devil, the setting is a baseball field. But it is reflective of a larger cosmic view—primarily held in the West—that our individual lives as well as the life of our world at large are being played out on a kind of a cosmic ball field or battlefield where the forces of God and the forces of Satan are contending for the upper hand.

It's a similar theme and imagery found in one of the *Star Wars* movies where the devil figure—in this case, Darth Vader—informs the virtuous Luke Skywalker that he (Luke) is really his son and urges him to "come over to the dark side." The not-so-subtle message is that we're all susceptible, having something of the devil in each us, to going over to the forces of evil—which is to say, to the devil's domain.

Exactly when this worldview began to take shape is hard to determine. In the Western world, it goes back at least to the Zoroastrian religion of ancient Persia. In this place and time the world was seen as, again, a battleground between the forces of light led by the god Ahura Mazda and the prince of darkness named Arihman. Many of the images of God and the devil that came to be found in the Judaic and Christian faiths are reflective of this Zoroastrian influence to which the ancient Hebrews were exposed at the time of the Babylonian captivity some six centuries before the Common Era. While that may help to explain *how* we got some of our images of the devil (and God), it still begs the larger question of *why* these images and why belief in the devil persists.

Persist it does. In a 2016 Gallup poll on American's religious views, 61 percent acknowledged belief in the devil. God does considerably better with an 89 percent belief rating. How the respondents to this poll actually conceptualized God and the devil is left unsaid.

Beyond the imagery and beyond who believes what about who, the deeper issue is the age-old matter referred to in this chapter's opening paragraph of how we as human beings come to terms with the reality of human evil. We go back several years on this point to an article that ran in *Newsweek* magazine as the twentieth century was coming to an end. It was one of many "wrap up the century" pieces that were running at the time. After citing some of the really horrible events of the twentieth century—the Holocaust, a number of ethnic cleansing type of genocides, and the like—it ended on this note:

> Wherever we turn, the [twentieth] century now drawing to a close has witnessed evil on a scale unmatched by any other. In an earlier America, evidence such as this would have immediately evoked a name, a face[,] and an explanation: Satan's

> powerful domination over a sinful, fallen humanity. Today, evil is experienced as random and ordinary, devoid of cosmic significance.

True as I take those words to be in general, I'm not so sure I'll completely buy the last line. I think the persistence of the image of the devil in some form or another is because there's a part of us that cannot accept the idea of evil as "random and ordinary [and] devoid of cosmic significance." When we witness events as breathtakingly horrifying—such as the Holocaust or ethnic cleansing or mass starvation sometimes brought on by despotic rulers or any number of acts of terrorism—we cannot help but feel, at least, that maybe there's something bigger going on here than that of human beings behaving in horribly bad ways toward other human beings. Trying to make some kind of rational sense out of some of the more unspeakably evil deeds human beings are capable of doing to one another can leave one simply feeling overwhelmed.

For some, perhaps the only way to articulate such overwhelmed feelings is to speak of someone or something called the devil, even if one cannot say for sure just who or what the devil is. I wonder how many of those 61 percent responders in that Gallup poll who said they believed in the devil were really searching for some greater, cosmic, explanation for unspeakably terrible and human-generated deeds that defy any kind of rational explanation.

I'm not exactly sure how I would have responded if the Gallup poll people had approached me in their survey. For me, it would have been complicated. If the question is do I believe in an actual, literal creature or being called Satan or the devil or Lucifer or whatever other name may be used who is the ultimate source and cause of all evil, then my answer is a flat-out no. I believe, whether such can be fully explained or not, that human beings are at the heart of all human evil, just as I believe that human beings are at the heart of all human good.

But—and here's my caveat—I'm also aware that human language often fails us or comes up short on a literal level. We seem to need some way to give voice and meaning to what we "vaguely apprehend" as the words of one hymn put it. So as a metaphor or symbol for ungraspable evil, "the devil" works on that level just as the term *God* can metaphorically or symbolically work for that which is greater than we know but cannot adequately name.

I would guess that if I were to explain all that to pollsters, they would give me a funny look and move on, hoping to find someone else from whom they could at least get a straight answer. That is my problem with these kinds of yes-or-no polls. They leave little, if any, room for nuance or for deliberate thought.

So to pick up on a metaphorical, as opposed to literal, take on the devil, I turn once again to my departed ministerial colleague and friend Forrest Church. In the numerous books on liberal religion he published in his lifetime, one is called *The Devil and Doctor Church.* In it he notes, "The Devil's trademark is not evil dressed as evil, but evil dressed as good. . . . [The Devil's] most successful ruse is to cloak himself in virtue."

Forrest is on to something here. Some of the most terrible deeds human beings have done to one another are those that have been, in his words, "cloaked in virtue." In order for certain kinds of evil to be perpetuated or, if you will, for the devil to do his work, a sense of unquestioned "rightness" or virtue needs to prevail. Such a sense of rightness may prevail only in the mind of a single individual, or it could be within a close circle of individuals as function of group-think—such as a terrorist cell—or it can be found within the mentality of a culture itself.

This angle on evil is well substantiated in Dr. Jessica's Stern's book *Terror in the Name of God.* Dr. Stern is a scholar and an academic on the subject of terrorism. She's a research professor at the Pardee School of Global Studies at Boston University and a former lecturer at Harvard University.

In researching her book, Dr. Stern was able to gain access to people who have perpetuated various kinds of terrorism, ranging from Al Qaeda operatives in the aftermath of 9/11, to people who target abortion providers to kill them, and to people who bomb abortion clinics. A more updated version of Dr. Stern's book could well include ISIS operatives and people who generate hatred toward LGBTQ individuals. In all such cases, those who perpetuate the terror or the hatred truly feel that they are in the service of righteousness; that they are, in Dr. Church's words, "cloaked in virtue."

This is why I forthrightly identify myself as a moral relativist, given that the alternative is moral absolutism. While moral absolutism does not fully explain or fully come to terms with the problem of evil, it goes a long way as an explanation, nonetheless. Moral absolutism can be found at the heart of many of the wars human beings have waged—often with those on both sides convinced of the moral rightness of their warring ways. It is at the heart of any number of heinous acts of torture and execution over the course of human history. It can be found in the hearts of those who hold signs reading "God hates fags" or in the rantings of some so-called preachers preaching hatred of Muslims. But it is not religion, as such, that lies at the heart of these kinds of evils—as some claim—but rather the religious, or moral, absolutism of those who perpetuate such evil.

As disparaged as the term is, I take and affirm moral relativism to mean that one makes their moral choices and courses of action *relative to* the circumstances and conditions within which a moral choice or course of action is called for. I have a number of strong opinions and convictions, and I hold those opinions and act on those convictions as I deem fit and proper. I also seek to guard against the malady of moral absolutism by examining my motives and the grounds for my opinions and convictions, often in conversation with those whose judgment and honesty I trust.

I said that moral absolutism or evil deeds cloaked in virtue do not fully explain or resolve the problem of evil itself. My most memorable and heart-wrenching exposure to the workings of evil was one that combined the result of moral absolutism with the unfathomable workings of—for lack of better terminology—a sick and hate-filled mind. It happened on a hot July afternoon in the summer of 2015 in Oklahoma City, Oklahoma. I'd offered the sermon at the Sunday morning service at Oklahoma City's Unitarian Universalist Church after attending the annual Woody Guthrie Festival a few days prior in Woody's hometown of Okemah, Oklahoma.

I wasn't flying back east until the following day and had that Sunday afternoon to myself. I drove over to the memorial site on the grounds that once housed the Alfred P. Murrah Federal Building. This was the building that was blown to smithereens on April 19, 1995, by a truck bomb built by Timothy McVeigh and Terry Nichols. It was McVeigh who drove the truck, parked it next to the building, and set the fuse for the explosion.

In addition to the complete destruction of the Murrah Building, several surrounding buildings also suffered great damage. McVeigh timed his terrorist attack for when the federal employees would be arriving for work. One hundred and sixty-eight people were killed by the blast. McVeigh was caught, tried, and eventually executed for his evil deed. Terry Nichols is serving several life sentences in an Oklahoma penitentiary.

I walked around the reflecting pool and stood before the 168 memorial chairs. I visited some of the displays that could be seen in one of the adjacent buildings that had been partially bombed, with some of the wreckage still left visible—looking as it had in the immediate aftermath of the bombing.

But what stopped me in my tracks was a photo exhibit of nineteen young children and toddlers. I hadn't planned it that way, but seeing this particular exhibit turned out to be my last stop at the memorial. I had to leave after that, unable to bear anymore. Of the 168 human beings killed by that terrorist blast were those nineteen kids. They were staying at an on-site childcare center in the Murrah Building for the employees who worked there. I looked at the pictures of those smiling, happy youngsters. I was riveted to the spot, even as I was at that Big Sur experience as described earlier.

But this time, instead of being riveted by the beauty of Big Sur, I was riveted by the presence of evil—not a presence, to be sure, in the faces of those beautiful and holy children but riveted by the presence and the force of the evil that took their lives. In my head, I remain an opponent of capital punishment for more reasons that I'll elaborate on here. Yet in my gut, standing before the pictures of those children, I felt Timothy McVeigh got what he deserved. But that's my dilemma to deal with.

A man whose over-the-top hatred of the government—the Bureau of Alcohol, Firearms, and Tobacco in particular—and his racism as generated by such hate-filled publications as *The Turner Diaries* and by his involvement in certain "Christian Identity" groups committed the greatest act of domestic terrorism in our nation's history. To know that is one thing; to witness some of the outcome of it up close face-to-face is another matter altogether.

The bombing of the Murrah Building can be attributed in part to the kind of moral absolutism as described earlier, in that Timothy McVeigh was convinced of the moral rightness of his deed. But it cannot be reduced to that. The workings of a sociopathic or psychopathic mind can perhaps be explained on a behavioral level, but we've yet to go much deeper than that. And while the image of the devil may have, as previously noted, some metaphorical value, there is no actual evil being at whose feet we can lay evil deeds. Maybe all we really are left with is what that *Newsweek* article suggested—"Today evil is experienced as random and ordinary, devoid of cosmic significance."

Cosmic significance or not, what we can do is maintain a heightened awareness of how we respond to the perpetuation of evil. We can heed the words of Simone Weil: "Never react to an evil in such a way as to augment it." She is saying that we cannot allow ourselves to be so overwhelmed by the presence of certain evil deeds that we end up going over "to the dark side" ourselves in attempting to do battle with it. Here we can take a cue from Martin Luther King: "I have decided to stay with love. Hatred is too great a burden to bear." Reverend King was not talking about a sentimental kind of love, but rather a love that calls us to redouble our efforts to create a sane, just, peaceful, and beloved community in the face of all that would weigh against such. And sometimes our broader vision of a beloved community can find its expression in simple—but not really simple—deeds of love and kindness.

It is the responses of the human spirit to what Abraham Lincoln called the *better angels of our nature* in the face of evil, or of the deeds of the devil—if you prefer that language, that offer a saving grace. I am still moved by a piece the actor Kirk Douglas wrote for the op-ed page of the *New York Times* many years ago. In this piece, Douglas told of being in Berlin to receive a lifetime achievement award and of his mixed feelings as a Jew about being there given that city's history within his own lifetime. But then he told about how, on this trip, he and his wife had dinner with a Jewish woman in Berlin whose parents and grandparents had died in the death camps. Mr. Douglas asked his hostess why she'd stayed in Berlin over the ensuing course of her life. This is how Kirk Douglas described the conversation that followed:

> Smiling, she gave me this answer: "I owe that to the little heroes."
>
> "I don't understand," I said. With a sigh, she came over and sat closer.
>
> "When the Gestapo came to get them, my parents sent me to a small hotel to save my life. The owner was the first little hero. She kept me safe for a couple of nights. When it became dangerous, I met my second little hero. Or should I say heroine? She was our former housekeeper. She hid me for a while and endangered her own life. Then I found a cloister. My little heroes were the nuns who took care of me when I was very sick. They never asked questions. When [my] situation [again] became dangerous, my next little hero was a policeman who didn't agree with the Nazis. All through the war, I was lucky to find little heroes who helped me till the Russians came in. . . . [I've stayed in Berlin because] I feel I owe it to the little heroes who helped me. Not everyone here was wicked."

Mr. Douglas then concluded, "Her story had a great impact on me. Of course, we're always looking for a big hero to emulate, and very often we see them topple from clay feet. How much better to reach for the little heroes in life—and try to be one."

The rise and onslaught of Nazism was among the greater evils of the previous century—an evil cloaked in the so-called good or virtue of creating a "master race" of white Arians. It still stands as a stark and scary example of how the forces of evil can almost overwhelm an entire society and culture. But as Kirk Douglas's story demonstrates, the operative word there is *almost.* "Not everyone was wicked," one of the survivors of that era noted. I doubt that those who came to the aid of the woman—then a young girl—who told her story to Kirk Douglas thought of themselves as heroes or heroines. They probably saw themselves as ordinary people who found themselves living in an extraordinary time and who were simply trying to do the right thing. Can any of us do any less?

I think this is what ultimately keeps evil—or the devil, so to speak—from having the final word: people who do the right thing at the right time in the face of whatever inhumane deed or whatever kind of inhumanity is being perpetuated; people who can still see the essential humanity in the eyes, faces, and hearts of their fellow human beings and respond accordingly when their humanity is being denied or diminished.

Recall again those words of Mahatma Gandhi: "Whatever you do may seem insignificant, but it is important that you do it anyway." However great the evil may be, no deed of love or kindness done in its face is insignificant.

Chapter 8

The Bible and I

I cannot write of my religious and spiritual odyssey without giving attention to the role the Bible has played in it. My ever-evolving understanding of the Bible is part and parcel of my ever-evolving spirituality. Beyond the personal, the impact of the Bible flows through the social, cultural, and political waters in which we all swim—even for those who have never even opened the book. I jump in with an incident that still gives me a good laugh, more than fifty years after it happened.

It was the greatest setup line I've ever handed anyone. It occurred near the end of my last year of college. I was home for a weekend. I went to the church of my upbringing for a Sunday-school class. By now I was old enough for the young-adult class that was a mix of college kids and others who had gone from graduating high school into jobs of one kind or another.

As I've noted in other places, the four years I spent in college remain the four most singularly transformative ones of my life. To be sure, there have been an ocean of life changes for me since then. But in terms of where my thinking and believing were when I was a freshman at age eighteen compared to when I graduated just short of my twenty-second birthday, I did more one-eighties in that span of time than in any other similar stretch of time in my life since then.

I was still as interested as ever in matters of religion and theology, all mixed in with a love for literature I'd developed as an English major. My plans for the ministry remained well in place. But, especially with this being the mid-1960s, I'd become fascinated with some of the latest trends in theological thinking. I no longer regarded such matters as "the death of God," which was getting some good press at the time, as a threat to my faith but rather as an invitation to explore the nature of my faith more fully. And I'd been accepted into one of the country's more liberal, academically oriented mainline Protestant theological seminaries. To all that high-minded stuff, I should add that I'd also become something of a wise guy, with an "I'm out of here" attitude toward the southern West Virginian culture in which I'd lived all my life up to then.

It was my wise-guy, know-it-all attitude that I took the young-adult Sunday-school class. I must have been spoiling for an argument. I have absolutely no memory of what the lesson was about, but the man who was teaching the class was using the word *God* in practically every sentence he spoke. It was "God says this" and "God wants that" and "God has commanded us to do this and such" and on and on. Finally, unable to restrain my self-assured self any longer, I piped up and said, "Well, it sounds to me like you've got God in your hip pocket."

I swear, the guy reached behind his back, pulled a small print Bible out of the rear pocket of his pants, and waved it at me as if it were a sharpened saber aimed at my head. He got his Bible right up under my nose and began yelling at me, "Yes, indeed, I do have God right here—right here in my hip pocket!" As I said, it was the best opening I've ever given anyone in my life, albeit one entirely at my expense.

Since the teacher was having so much fun with the line I'd handed him and since I still had enough respect for the larger setting in which this little episode was taking place, I figured my best move was to lose my wise-guy act and just let it go—which I did. I imagine this gentleman went to his Sunday dinner that day, very pleased with himself for having told that smart-ass college boy a thing or two. Well, I doubt he would have used a term such as "smart-ass." He was too good a Baptist for that.

Giving credit where it's due, this Sunday-school teacher gave me something of value. What I got that Sunday morning was one of the several indicators I'd already received at that point in my life, telling me that it was time to move on. A geographical move was already in the works that would take me several hundred miles north to Rochester, New York. But it was also a major rearranging of my religious and spiritual views at age twenty-two that was pointing me in that direction. While much of my impending move felt like an escape ("I am out of here!"), I was also leaving—as I had to admit to myself—with a certain respect for all that had gotten me to the age of eighteen, as well as a strong appreciation for the many challenges to my faith that had come in the three to four years after that.

Some of what was pointing me on my way had to do with how I'd come to read and understand the Bible. It wasn't just a rhetorical flourish that "God in my hip pocket" gentleman was engaging in. He was reflecting quite well the ethos of the religious milieu I was brought up in, where God and the Bible were practically synonymous. At a later point in my life, I would conclude that the God-Bible equation was, and is, a form of idolatry, but I hardly felt that way in my early years.

To grow up in the near-but-not-quite Christian fundamentalist setting that I did means, among other things, that you are given a lens through which you are expected to read the Bible before you really know what all is in it. Part of my larger journey of faith and meaning has involved changing the lenses through which I read the Bible. And while this text is no longer central to my ongoing faith formation, I have not cast it aside. The various biblical allusions I use in this book attest to that.

To begin at the beginning, my initial lens for Bible reading was that it is the inerrant divinely inspired Word of God—every bit of it from Genesis 1:1 to Revelation 22:21. "Cover to cover," the expression goes. I was given a little wriggle room here and there—that is, maybe the "day" in the first chapter of Genesis doesn't mean a specific twenty-four–hour stretch of time. But in a larger sense, what the Bible said was "God's Word," no argument and no exceptions. One thing I still value about first reading the Bible through such a lens is that it made me biblically literate, which remains a good thing for me to be as I travel through my various ports of call.

The next biblical lens I got began working its way into my consciousness toward the latter part of my college years in some of the philosophy and religion courses I took as they were taught in a secular university. I came to see that, rather than being a single text, the Bible was actually more of an anthology written over a period of several centuries by a wide variety of authors, none of whom had the faintest idea that what they were writing would one day appear in a single work called the Bible. By the time I got out of college, I'd come to view the Bible as a human document written over a span of time by many human beings whose writings reflected the historical context and culture within which they wrote as well as their motivations and their agendas for writing what they did.

So what happened to the "Word of God"? Here I got some help from a very fine New Testament professor at my seminary. He taught that the Bible is a compilation of *words* that point us toward the *Eternal Word.* He used the first verse of the New Testament Gospel of John to make his point: "In the beginning was The Word [i.e., God]." The Bible, as he taught it, was a record of human attempts to create the *words* that would gain us a clearer understanding of *the Word*. The *words* of the Bible were a fair game for any kinds of critiques or analyses we wanted to give them based on the best biblical research and scholarship available so long as we held on to the idea that there was an *Eternal Word* toward which these *words* were directing us. So biblical criticism was all well and good and even expected while still being carried forth in a setting that was preparing people for the Christian ministry.

That biblical lens got me through seminary, past my ordination review board, and into my early years in the liberal Christian ministry. But when I began to probe more deeply into what this "Eternal Word" was really all about, I found less value in the words-and-Word lens. The lenses I've used since then in my reading of the Bible are less definitive than these first two, and I'll come to them at later points in this chapter. As noted above, I still find value and inspiration from various parts of the Bible, but it is no longer central for me as I continue along making my "human response to the dual reality of being alive and knowing I will die." (Thank you, Forrest.)

I've come to see that the presence and power of the Bible is something that flows through the cultural, societal, and political waters in which we all swim. Whatever one's personal way of relating to the Bible may be—or even if there is no relationship at all—we all still swim in those waters.

For a closer look at those waters and the role of the Bible within them, consider the following:

The largest Protestant denomination in the United States is the Southern Baptist Convention (SBC). It has over forty-six thousand congregations in the United States and beyond, with approximately fifteen million members. I cite these numbers to indicate that I am not lifting up some obscure sect or cult in considering the role of the Bible in our larger society. I am going instead to our largest American Protestant Christian denomination that is second only to the Catholic Church when it comes to the largest Christian body in America. One of the largest churches in the SBC is the First Baptist Church (FBC) of Dallas, Texas, with a membership of over ten thousand. Its minister, as of this writing, is Rev. Robert Jeffress.

The position of FBC Dallas on the Bible as shown on the Church's website is clear and straightforward: "We believe that all Scripture in divinely inspired and serves as the final authority in all matters of belief and practice." Try it again for good measure: "We believe that all Scripture is divinely inspired and serves as the final authority in all matters of belief and practice." This is the lens through which the Bible is viewed and read in America's largest Protestant Christian body.

Given this kind of prominence, FBC Dallas's senior minister Reverend Jeffress also holds a certain level of national prominence. He's one of the "go to" people who get called on when the national media—usually Fox News or CNN—are looking for a weigh in from someone espousing so-called biblical values when it comes to a social issue of one kind or another. This has given Reverend Jeffress a national forum to express his opposition to same-sex marriage or to any positive portrayal of LGBTQ people, to his denunciations of Islam as an "evil . . . violent . . . [and] false" religion, to his pronouncement that the course in which former President Obama was leading the nation "is paving the way for the future reign of the anti-Christ."

That's just Rev. Jeffress's short list. To reiterate what has been noted, these statements are not being made by an obscure cult figure leading some obscure cultic sect. They are being offered up instead, with the help of the national media, by the senior minister of one of the largest churches affiliated with America's largest Protestant Christian body. He claims that in saying the things that he does, he is upholding "biblical values." These values are derived from the biblical lens cited on the FBC Dallas website: "We believe that *all Scripture* is divinely inspired and serves as *the final authority* in *all matters* of belief and practice [emphasis added]."

Those words may be on the Church's website, but I fail to see how its senior minister, or any minister who reads the Bible through such a lens, or any layperson for that matter, can, in good faith and conscience, actually believe them. For example, among the verses in the Old Testament that condemn homosexuality, which I'm sure Reverend Jeffress and his Southern Baptist minister colleagues have no hesitation in citing, is also one that stipulates that a woman who is not a virgin at the time of her marriage is to be stoned to death. That would be Deuteronomy 22:20–21. I wonder when was the last time Reverend Jeffress or any of his SBC ministerial colleagues preached a sermon on that "divinely inspired" and "final authority" passage. Try never.

To move to the New Testament, we find a passage where Jesus says that anyone—of either sex—who divorces and remarries has committed adultery. That would be the Gospel of Mark 10:11–12. Surely, among those ten thousand members of the First Baptist Church of Dallas, as well as the members of those forty-six thousand SBC churches across our country's religious landscape, are men and women who have divorced and remarried. When do you suppose was the last time any of their ministers called these folks out as adulterers? Try never.

If you can stand this riff any longer, we go to the passage in the New Testament Book of First Timothy, right there in the second chapter that says that women are to keep silent in the church and can only be instructed by men. Surely, among those ten thousand members of FBC Dallas are females—as there are in all those other forty-six thousand SBC Churches. When do you suppose was the last time any of their ministers told the women in their congregations to zip their lips as soon as they walked through the doors of their church and keep them that way until they left? And oh yes, dear ladies, you are only to be instructed by men. One more time—try never.

So what gives here? Are some "biblical values" more "biblical" than others? But how can that be if *all Scripture* constitutes the *final authority* in *all matters* of belief and practice? Hence my point—such a statement about this particular lens cannot be fully believed or seriously taken. I say "cannot be fully believed" since what those who supposedly wear this particular biblical lens really do is pick the verses that cater to their sociopolitical agendas and quietly overlook the rest.

It is time to leave the Southern Baptists to their doings and take a quick look at America's larger religious landscape. According to polls taken by the Gallup organization in 2016 and 2017, 24 percent of Americans regard the Bible as the actual, literal "Word of God." This is actually down from the 40 percent who stated such a belief in 1984. At the other end of the spectrum, 26 percent take the Bible to be a mix—or hodgepodge, if you will—of secular stories, history, fables, legends, myths, and moral precepts. The larger middle ground, with 47 percent, regard the Bible as the "inspired Word of God" but with a fair amount of room left for interpreting just what "inspired Word of God" means and with not all the interpretations being the same. What this suggests to me is that in our overall sociocultural landscape, there is no one overriding set of lenses through which Americans view the Bible. We tend to be all over the place.

Another angle for approaching an understanding of the Bible, alongside the lens approach I've been taking, is to think in terms of the Bible as a book or text, or the Bible as an icon. The two overlap in a number of ways, but a distinction can still be made. Taken as a book or as a collection of writings in the manner suggested earlier, the Bible is a compendium of works—some of them magnificent and lofty and wonderful, and some are downright horrible.

The text of the document now known as the Bible evolved over the first few centuries of the Christian Church. As Christian communities came into being around the lands bordering the Mediterranean Sea, a variety of accounts of the life and ministry of Jesus and a variety of letters of certain Apostles as well as various other documents came to be viewed as authoritative in different ones of those communities. But there was no one single text that was regarded as binding, or authoritative, for all those early Christian communities.

A few centuries went by. In the year 325, Christianity became the official religion of the Roman Empire, following the conversion of the emperor Constantine. This allowed the Christian Church to centralize its power and authority in Rome. A centralized church needed a centralized canon to say what constituted "holy scripture" and what did not.

To this end, in the year 382, Pope Damascus I convened the Council of Rome. It was this council that decreed which books would constitute the Christian Bible. They were, by and large, the books that had come to be generally recognized by then as authoritative throughout the Christian world. The Council of Rome, for the most part, was putting the church's seal of approval on what had been evolving for over three centuries. The twenty-seven books that make up the New Testament today are the same ones that were canonized by the Council of Rome. Protestants and Catholics differ slightly on which of the canonical books—as also decreed by the Council of Rome—constitute the Old Testament.

The proceedings of the Council of Rome are a matter of historical record, whatever one's view of the content of the Bible the council brought into being. I cite all this to point out that what is now called the New Testament of the Bible was not fully and finally set in place until 350 years after Jesus's earthly ministry.

That is the Bible as text. Then there is the Bible as an icon, or totem, called THE BIBLE in all capital letters. This totemic status of the Bible actually transcends the text. The best way for me to explain this totemic status is to tell another story. I remember it as clearly as the one about the Sunday-school teacher with "God" in his hip pocket. This one came many years later when I was serving a Unitarian Universalist congregation on New York's Long Island.

In the final months of my ministry there, a rather quiet and retiring gentleman began attending the worship services. I was able to draw him out a bit in a conversation during the coffee hour that followed a service one Sunday. As we talked, he told me about how he and his wife were members of a very evangelical and near-fundamentalist congregation (I knew the territory) with which he was coming to feel increasingly disaffected. His wife, on the other hand, was a very devout and committed believer in the religion of that church. As one might imagine, this was creating some tension in their marriage.

One Sunday, a few weeks later, he managed to convince his wife to come to a service with him. Maybe he wanted to show her he wasn't getting sucked into some weirdo cult with a wacky cult leader. ("See, honey, that minister up there is just an ordinary guy.") They sat right in the front row.

I was in the pulpit, holding forth on a pretty basic Unitarian Universalist type of sermon when I noticed this gentleman's wife was clutching a Bible right over her heart. Her knuckles were white, the same way many of our knuckles get white when we clutch the side of an airplane seat if the plane encounters turbulence. She stayed in a white-knuckle-on-the-Bible mode throughout the sermon. Even though I wasn't doing or saying anything hostile or threatening—certainly not deliberately—I'm quite sure she felt as if she were in a hostile and threatening environment and that if she just held on to her Bible tightly enough, she would come through it and still be okay.

I cite this story not to mock or denigrate this woman's faith. I grew up with folks like her. They are, for the most part, good and honest and decent-minded people. They are people who sometimes feel they are living in a world that is hostile to their faith, and the Bible is the iconic shield they hold up against that perceived hostility.

My ministry with that Long Island congregation came to an end shortly after this incident, and I never learned what became of that couple. But seeing this devout woman clutching her Bible as if it were a life preserver—which for her it probably was—while I was delivering a sermon is an image from my ministry that has long stayed with me.

So yes, I understand the Bible's iconic or totemic status that transcends the text while still making use of it. This iconic status can be used as either an instrument of oppression or one of liberation. On the oppressive side, if same sex-marriage—now legal by rule of the United States

Supreme Court—poses an imagined threat to all that is right and good about our society, then the verses that condemn homosexuality will be extracted and held up in order that "biblical values" may be maintained.

It's an old tune. It's the verses that change from one age to the next. During the abolitionist movement, there were devout folks who saw the denial of legal standing to slavery as a threat to the established order. They took their biblical text from the Book of Timothy in a passage that reads, "Those who are under the yoke of slavery must regard their masters worthy of full respect" (1 Timothy 6:1). According to this particular text, the abolitionists were "unbiblical" and the supporters of slavery were upholding "biblical values."

Another verse in this tune played out during the women's suffrage movement. Given the host of Bible verses that call for the subjugation of women—some of which we've already seen—the full enfranchisement of women was deemed contrary to biblical values.

Whether it was to support the institution of slavery or to keep women in their so-called place or to attempt to deny basic human rights to LGBTQ people, the use of the Bible's iconic status has long been employed to substantiate bigotry or moral shortsightedness.

Alongside such efforts to use the Bible's iconic status to resist some of the nineteenth century's moves for greater levels of social justice, there were also devout Christians who used their understanding of Christianity and their reading of the Bible to support and advance such moves. One of the leading lights of the abolitionist movement was the Boston-based Unitarian minister Rev. Theodore Parker who took his Bible seriously. Among the more high-profile leaders of the women's suffrage movement were Susan B. Anthony and Elizabeth Cady Stanton, both strong Christian women who also took their Bible as seriously as their opponents did.

Be that as it may, the invocation of the Bible to thwart some of these movements for social justice can, in good measure, be traced to the late nineteenth and early twentieth centuries in America, with the simultaneous rise of modernism and Protestant Christian fundamentalism. Fundamentalism in America is not an "old-time religion" when put in the context of over two thousand years of Christianity in the West. Western-style Christian fundamentalism only took shape about a century and a half ago. It arose in reaction to a host of modernistic ideas that were erupting at roughly the same time. They included Darwinism and the posting of the theory of evolution, the scientific age in general, the beginnings of the drive for women's equality, the advent of psychology and psychological analysis, and the use of modern biblical analysis and criticism in America's more liberal theological seminaries.

In the face of all this change and upheaval, certain sectors of American Protestantism reacted much in the same way as the woman at that Sunday service on Long Island. They made the Bible into totem, a supposedly solid rock standing against the shifting sands of modernism. For the Fundamentalists, this move included an insistence upon the verbal inerrancy of the Bible where there had not been such an adamant insistence previously. This was when the Bible went from being honored and respected—as I feel it should, by and large, be—to being made into an idol or into a bulwark that could be held up to guard against a radically changing world. This was an effort that succeeded in part and continues to fuel the cultural wars and struggles that persist to the day.

Note I said "succeeded in part." It was the rise of Fundamentalism that greatly precipitated the Fundamentalist-Modernist split that ran through American Protestantism in the early twentieth century. And this split was largely around how the Bible was to be read and interpreted—which lens to use, that is. While the Modernists still regarded the Bible as the "Word of God" along the lines I got in my seminary in the 1960s, they were open to reading and understanding its passages within the historical and cultural contexts of which they were written, and then sought to apply them accordingly to the present age. All this to say that the iconic status of the Bible gets played out clear across the fundamentalist or conservative to liberal or radical spectrum of American Protestant Christianity.

This gets me back to the lens through which I read the Bible in this "post-Christian" phase of my life. It's an expansion of the lens I received all those many years ago in theological school but one that does not concern itself so much with that "words or Word" construct.

I have come to view the Bible as an account of the human search for the divine, the sacred, the holy—or call it *God* if you prefer—rather than a text authored by God for us human beings in some way or another. Some of those human searches for the divine were noble ones; others were terrible failures. Put another way the Bible is a human record of the efforts of human beings who were trying to reach beyond themselves for whatever they sensed was greater than themselves. They gave this "greater thing" many names: God, Jehovah, Yahweh, the Lord, to cite a few.

Some of the qualities and activities that became attributed to this God are horrific, if not terroristic. There are the bloody massacres done in the name of Yahweh and recorded in the book of Joshua, for example. That was one of those terribly failed searches to which I just referred. Other such failures are the portrayals of an avenging, judging, minute law-giving, and sometimes petulant God that show up in the Old Testament or, for that matter, of a God who requires the blood sacrifice of His own Son for the sake of the fallen humanity in the New Testament. Failures all.

At the same time, there are also many noble and enlightened biblical efforts to imagine the divine or the sacred. There are the stories of the Hebrew prophets calling in the name of Yahweh for a more just and humane society. There are the stories of the prophet Amos standing in the town squares of his day, calling out, "Let justice roll down like waters and righteousness like a mighty stream."

Then there is Jesus, another of the Hebrew prophets really, who—also in the name of the god he usually called *Father*—taught the ways of love and kindness and compassion and healing. These are traits that represent some of the best of our human efforts to find what Abraham Lincoln called *the better angels of our nature.*

The stories in the book of Exodus, interwoven as they are with a tribalistic and nationalistic kind of God also tell of the struggles of escape from human bondage and the attainment of human liberation. It is a narrative that strikes a universal human chord for freedom everywhere. The Exodus story was one that Martin Luther King often invoked as a metaphor for the struggles of the civil rights movement.

Dr. King also invoked biblical imagery in his best-known speech given on August 28, 1963, at the Lincoln Memorial with these words: "I have a dream that one day every valley shall be exalted, every hill and mountain shall be made low, the rough places shall be made plain, and the crooked places shall be made straight and the glory of the Lord will be revealed and all flesh shall see it together. This is our hope."

Reverend King was citing a passage from the fortieth chapter of the book of Isaiah. He knew of the iconic status the Bible held in much of America's Afro-American community, and he was speaking the language of that community. He invoked yet another biblical image on the night before he was murdered when he said, "I have been to the mountain top, and I have seen the Promised Land." Here he was referring to a passage in the Exodus narrative where Moses is allowed to see the land where he is leading his people but he will die before entering it. Here again, Reverend King was speaking to an audience who was familiar with that passage and knew what he was talking about.

The Bible is indeed a powerful text. It is a text that can be used as an instrument of oppression or one of liberation, depending upon whose hand the text is in and with whose voice it is spoken.

What I see in the Bible is a progression. It is not a straight-line progression by any means but a progression, nonetheless, from the portrayals of a very narrow, if not dangerous, kind of God to one that embodies certain universal human values. The Bible is not so much about God as it is about human beings trying to discover a greater meaning and purpose—a greater holy and sacred meaning—in their lives and in the world where they lived using the term *God* among other names.

I don't have "God" in my hip pocket or anywhere else for that matter. But I get some help now and then from the Bible in my ongoing pursuit of "that which is greater than all and present in all."

Chapter 9
A Meditation on the Holy

In the summer of 1955, Allen Ginsberg was a twenty-seven-year-old aspiring poet, but still not widely published. He'd spent all his life to that point in the New York City area and was now giving San Francisco a try. Several years earlier, he'd been treated at the New York Psychiatric Institute for various mental and emotional difficulties. The advice he was given by those treating him was that he needed to suppress his homosexuality, divest himself of his fringy bohemian friends, get himself a girlfriend, and attempt to live a "normal" life in accordance with the norms of mainstream American society in the early 1950s. This was considered a sound psychiatric advice at the time.

At the outset of the West Coast phase of his life, Allen decided to give that advice a try. He got a copywriting job for a marketing agency, put on a coat and tie, carried a briefcase to work, and got himself a girlfriend. It was a nice try, but it didn't work. In the spring of 1955, he met a young man named Peter Orlovsky. They began what became a lifelong partnered relationship, albeit one with its numerous complications.

Allen also decided that the lifestyle he was attempting to cultivate was, in effect, destroying his soul. He further decided that, contrary to the opinions of those who had treated him some years earlier, the real madness, or craziness, was not within him but within a larger culture that demanded he live his life in ways that were becoming increasingly alien to him. He lost the job, lost the girlfriend, and decided to risk taking up Thoreau's call to march to the beat of one's own drummer.

So it was in that summer of 1955 while sharing an apartment with Peter in San Francisco, Allen began writing a long epic-style poem that began with the words "I saw the best minds of my generation destroyed by madness," and it went from there. He sent a copy of his then untitled work to his friend Jack Kerouac who replied in a letter, "I read your howl." Ginsberg decided that was a pretty good title for his screaming poem about all he saw and believed was driving him and his contemporaries crazy. Many decades later, the poem that launched Allen Ginsberg's literary career—with the help of an obscenity trial following its initial publication—has found its way into many anthologies of American poetry and literature.

Between the time he first publicly read *Howl* at a gathering of poets in the fall of 1955 and when Lawrence Ferlinghetti's City Lights Press published it, Ginsberg added a couple of sections, with a conclusion called *Footnote to Howl.* This footnote begins with the word *holy* being repeated fifteen times, with an exclamation point after each *holy.*

Among its lines that I especially like are these:

> Holy the solitudes of skyscrapers and pavements! Holy the cafeterias filled with millions! Holy the mysterious rivers of tears under the streets!

It makes for an intriguing juxtaposition; Ginsberg seeing something he calls *holy* right in the very midst of all he perceived as being destructive of the soul.

There's a similar kind of destructive-holy dynamic going on in some of the songs and poems of Woody Guthrie, albeit in a very different kind of setting than those of Ginsberg's and on a much more literal level. While just barely out of his teens, and living in Pampa, Texas, after moving there from his hometown of Okemah, Oklahoma, Woody found himself eking out an existence with a young wife and a couple of kids. Then he witnessed the severe dust storms that blew across Oklahoma and Texas in the late 1920s, destroying what meager existence the folks making their living from the land in those parts had.

Many of Guthrie's dust bowl ballads described the terrible plight of people forced off their land who were moving westward—as Woody

Guthrie himself did—desperately seeking other ways of making a living and supporting their families.

But in the midst of all that desperation, Woody saw a certain kind of sacredness or holiness in the land he traveled, however severely beaten down it may have been in places. He wrote a song called "Holy Ground."

> Take off, take off your shoes.
> This place you're standing, it's holy ground…
> Every step you take is holy ground
> Every step is on holy ground.

Numerous other examples could be cited, but we'll leave it with Ginsberg and Guthrie. Examples, that is to say, of people with artistic, poetic, or literary sensitivities who seek and, at times, find a certain kind of sacred or holy dimension to life, even in the midst of all that diminishes or demeans life.

But one need not be in the ranks of poets and artists to see what many of them see and sense. The two examples I just cited point to a way of looking at the world—a lens through which to see all that we encounter. I've called this a religious lens—religious in the sense that it gives a certain kind of depth or deeper meaning to the lives we live and the settings in which we live them.

I find some good help when I get to thinking along these lines from a book by the late Dr. Marcus Borg, a biblical scholar and professor of religious studies, called *The God We Never Knew.* It was my privilege to take an intensive five-day seminar with Dr. Borg at the Pacific School of Religion several years before he passed away.

The Pacific School of Religion sits up in the lofty heights of the Berkeley Hills. It offers a beautiful panoramic view of much of the Bay Area. Whatever one's theology may be, it's a good place to think about God, a good place to sense the holy. That particular area of Berkeley, in fact, has several seminary campuses in it, which is why it is often referred to as Holy Hill.

To return to Dr. Borg, the story he tells in the opening chapter of his book has a familiar ring to it for me. He writes of how the childhood faith in which he was raised—in his case, it was Minnesota Lutheran and straight out of Garrison Keillor's Lake Wobegon—eventually went by the board for him. As he puts it, "By the time I was thirty, like Humpty Dumpty, my childhood faith had fallen to pieces." Unlike "all the king's horses and all the king's men," however, Borg was able to reconstruct his faith, albeit into a radically altered form.

What fell to pieces was what Borg calls *supernatural theism*, that is to say, God as a Supreme Being who exists outside the working of the natural world and universe and who can intervene—as He, She, or It chooses—in those workings. This is also the God I knew as I was growing up, and while He could be a punishing deity when it came to nonbelievers, the image I mostly got was a positive one.

But for all the comfort I derived from such a God at an earlier point in my life, I am now, and have been for some time, with Dr. Borg in saying that if the only belief-in-God possibility is that of supernatural theism, then I'd have to declare myself an atheist.

What Dr. Borg offers is an alternative to atheism—a "third way," if you will. He calls it *panentheism*. I introduced the term in an earlier chapter. Dr. Borg was the person who introduced it to me.

Panentheism, as previously noted, is not so much a definition of God as it is a description of those lenses through which we see the world that I referred to earlier in this chapter. It holds that there is something sacred or holy contained within the ordinary or the everyday, and if we stay open to it, that sacredness or holiness will, on occasion, break through. This is a perspective I take in my ongoing journey of faith as I try to keep focused on the challenge of walking through life and really seeing it.

The main difference between the panentheism of Dr. Borg and the panentheism I have come to is that Dr. Borg kept his theology within a liberal Christian context, while I do not. The person of Jesus for Dr. Borg remained central to his spirituality in that he saw in the image of Jesus an "exhibit A" example of someone who was fully in touch with his innate holiness. Dr. Borg, as one of the principal participants in the Jesus Seminar, knew that the actual human Jesus was largely lost in the historical mists. It was in the image of Jesus that Borg found his paradigm for panentheism. For those who wish to explore this perspective further, I recommend Dr. Borg's book *Meeting Jesus for the First Time.*

I have nothing by the highest respect and admiration for Marcus Borg's scholarship and theology. It's just that when it comes to my own embracing of panentheism, I do not view the image of Jesus through the same lens as he does. Nonetheless, Dr. Borg has been a major influence in my religious and spiritual journey.

I offer here yet another story from that journey, particularly as it relates to what I've taken from Borg's works. It's about one of the more profound experiences I've had over my years in the ministry:

A few weeks prior to my leaving for California to study with Dr. Borg, I was asked to officiate a funeral in Nashua at a funeral home not far from the church I was serving at the time. It was for a young man named Trent who had died homeless on the streets of San Francisco. He'd grown up in Nashua, and his parents, though divorced, wanted to have him buried in a family plot in the nearby town of Hollis.

In talking with the members of Trent's family, I learned of a very gifted and talented individual who, for whatever reasons, could not adapt himself to the usual patterns of living that most of us do. They acknowledged his struggles with alcohol. He was a very capable writer, and I was shown some articles he'd written about the homeless for some of San Francisco's more alternative style newspapers. He wrote with passion and anger and in a very unsentimental way.

Following the service, a gentleman who had driven up from Connecticut approached me. His daughter, a recent graduate of Boston College, was working for a human service agency in San Francisco. She'd known Trent. She'd even arranged for a memorial service to be held at the vacant lot where he usually slept, and she'd asked her father to attend the service in Nashua on her behalf.

When I told this gentleman that I'd be in the Bay Area later that summer, he gave me some contact information so that his daughter and I could meet. That was how I came to find myself a few weeks hence in the battered lobby of a battered store-front type of building that housed a human-service agency, asking for someone named Rose. People from the streets came in looking for leads on jobs, places to stay, any available assistance, and the like. It was, in more ways than one, a long, long way from the lofty and rarified heights of the Berkeley Hills where I was studying with Dr. Borg.

Rose and I began our walk. San Francisco is a beautiful city, but this was its underside—a place where no tourist map will direct you. We passed a line of people waiting to get into a church to be served a meal. We were stopped by someone with a story about why he needed money. In a calm, cheerful, but firm way, my walking companion told him where he needed to go to get the help he needed. She was pretty firm about not handing out cash. I'm not sure how I would have felt had I been taking this walk alone, but I felt completely at ease walking in the company of a young woman who was less than half my age.

We met a few people who had known Trent. She introduced me to them and told them I'd conducted his funeral back east in a town called Nashua, New Hampshire. They'd never heard of the place, but they thanked me. We came to a small vacant lot where a couple of buildings met at a right angle, a little ways back from the street. This, Rose told me, was where Trent lived—under a forlorn-looking tree. There was a pile of withered flowers still scattered around the trunk, placed there by friends a few weeks earlier. Rose asked if we could stand next to the tree and if I'd say a prayer for Trent. I was happy to oblige. It was one of the more moving experiences I've had in all my years in the ministry. Rose and I then walked back to where she worked and said our goodbyes. I drove back over the Bay Bridge and back up into the lofty Berkeley Hills.

The last thing I want to do is romanticize or sentimentalize homelessness or poverty as there's none to be had. There's no single explanation or culprit about why some people struggle for existence in the midst of the relative comfort most of us know. It's a tough and complex issue and not one to be easily untangled.

But what I saw on that short little journey was about more than struggles for material survival. It was that, but it was more than that. There was also a need and desire by companion and guide, as well as for those we met up with, to affirm a life that had touched others' lives—a life that had its own kind of sacredness and holiness, however broken it may have also been.

The withered flowers and the hard dirt at that site were evocative of those lines of Ginsberg's I cited earlier, "Holy the mysterious river of tears under the streets," as well as those of Woody Guthrie, "Every step you take is holy ground."

As I said earlier, I'm not putting forth a belief system with all this so much as I'm offering a lens through which we can look at the world around us. It's a lens that can open us up to both its beauty and its brokenness. It's the lens through which Albert Schweitzer looked when he proclaimed and lived out what he called a *reverence* for life. For seeking and, at times, finding an essential holiness or sacredness to life provides one a call to awareness and a call to response when that holiness is violated.

When people go hungry or are innocently caught in the ravages of war, the sacred, the holy, is violated. When the earth is despoiled by human greed and overreaching, the sacred is violated. When a person's essential human dignity is demeaned because of their race or gender or ethnicity or faith stance or sexual orientation or station in life, the sacred is violated. When we see the holy profaned or when we violate it ourselves, we are then called to renewal and to recommitment to be people of faith, in the best sense of the term—the faith that we can be agents of healing and reconciliation and transformation in the broken places of life.

There's a common message in the two settings I've described—the beauty of Holy Hill and the holiness beneath the river of tears of broken streets. The message is that contained within the beauty of life as well as contained within the meaner and crueler aspects of life is the truth that none of it is trivial. There is a presence, a power, a spirit within that ordinariness—even within that meanness—that can bless us and summon us to keep faith with the life we live and the life to which we aspire.

Chapter 10

A Meditation on Grace

The poem was written by Jane Kenyon. The title is "Otherwise"

I got out of bed
on two strong legs.
It might have been
otherwise. I ate
cereal, sweet
milk, ripe, flawless
peach. It might
have been otherwise.
I took the dog uphill
to the birch wood.
All morning I did
the work I love.

At noon I lay down
with my mate. It might
have been otherwise.
We ate dinner together
at a table with silver
candlesticks. It might
have been otherwise.
I slept in a bed
in a room with paintings
on the walls, and

planned another day
just like this day.
But one day, I know,
it will be otherwise.

This poem was published in 1996 as part of a collection by Ms. Kenyon titled *Otherwise: New and Selected Poems.* It was a posthumous publication. Ms. Kenyon died in 1995 from leukemia, one month short of her forty-eighth birthday. She was living with her husband, the poet Donald Hall, at their home in Wilmot, New Hampshire. Ms. Kenyon was the poet laureate of New Hampshire at the time of her death.

Like much of Ms. Kenyon's poetry, this poem of hers needs little interpretation. It's about grace. It is about finding gracious moments in what might be called the *profound ordinariness* of life. Such graceful times can indeed be amazing. One of the things that makes such times moments of grace is because we know, on some level, that they are only with us for—well, a moment, and then it will be otherwise. Indeed, Jane Kenyon wrote these words, knowing that "otherwise," in the most ultimate sense, was near at hand for her.

There is also an element of "letting go" here. Ms. Kenyon is also attempting to let go of what will, in time, be "otherwise" in order to be in a gracious moment.

While we may seek out gracious moments, the more likely occurrence is that they find us. Such, in fact, was the case behind the writing of the best known ode to grace, if you will. It is John Newton's well-known hymn "Amazing Grace."

"Amazing Grace" is an amazing song. It's probably the only hymn you'll find in the hymnals for both the Southern Baptists and the Unitarian Universalists. And while it is considered a Christian hymn, I find it a matter of curiosity that there is no reference anywhere in it to Jesus Christ. There's not even a reference to God—and a passing one at that—until you get to the fourth verse, and that verse wasn't part of the original version and was not written by the original author.

One of the most enduring recordings of the song was done way back in the day by Judy Collins who has no particular religious agenda I can detect. It became a countercultural ode when Arlo Guthrie sang it at Woodstock and then worked it into the *Alice's Restaurant* movie.

Moving to more recent times, the most moving moment of Barack Obama's presidency came when he sang this song as part of his eulogy at the memorial service held at the Emmanuel African Methodist Episcopal Church in Charleston, South Carolina, to honor the lives of those killed in a vicious, racially motivated hate crime. The dead included the church's minister, the Reverend Clementia Pickney, and eight lay members.

What is it then about this song that gives it such a universal appeal?

The account of how "Amazing Grace" came to be written is a good starting point and a good story all by itself. It's the story of John Newton, born in London in 1725. He went to sea at age eleven with his father after his mother died. During his life at sea, he became, by most accounts, a real wretch. He was just not a nice person.

On one of his voyages, his fellow sailors actually complained to the captain about Newton's prolific and excessive swearing. Imagine that: a ship full of sailors upset at a shipmate's swearing. The crew of yet another ship, the *Pegasus,* became so put out with him that they left him in West Africa with one of the slave dealers with whom they were working as part of the slave trade. This resulted in Newton's being held in virtual enslavement himself until he was rescued by another ship.

In time, however, he became an accomplished enough sailor so that by the time he reached his early twenties, he was the captain of his own ship—a slave ship, in this case—transporting captured Africans to America to be sold into slavery.

Then in an account with "Jonah and the Whale" overtones, on a voyage that took place in March of 1748, Newton's ship came into a violent storm that no one on board thought they were going to survive. As he tried to steer his ship through the storm, not knowing where he was or where he was going, Newton realized he'd come to one of those "let go and let God" moments—to use a little 12-step language—a moment, that is to say, when he realized that his life and his fate were no longer in his hands; that they were instead in the hand of a power or powers greater than himself. All he could do was to let go and let life (or death) happen.

The ship and crew survived, and Captain Newton had a religious conversion that, over the course of the following years, eventually resulted in his becoming the Reverend John Newton, an Anglican minister. His conversion was not a one-time event. After his near death at sea, Newton gave up his swearing, drinking, and gambling, but he did not leave the slave trade until 1754 when he gave up seafaring and pursued the Anglican ministry. He did not fully denounce the slave trade until much later in his life by finally declaring himself an abolitionist.

As Reverend Newton, he became a prolific hymn writer up until his death at age eighty-two. "Amazing Grace" was one of the hymns contained in a volume of his work that was published in 1779. Its actual title was "Faith's Review and Expectation" with "Amazing Grace" being the opening words. There is some speculation—although never fully established—that Newton got the tune for "Amazing Grace" from listening to the singing of the captives he was transporting on his slave ships.

In some respects, the song hearkens back to Newton's seafaring conversion experience in some quite literal ways: "I once was lost but now I'm found. . . . 'Twas grace that brought me safe this far and grace will lead me home. . . . Through many dangers toils and snares, I have already come."

That's the story anyway. But how do we account for the staying power of a hymn written some 250 years ago by a slave trader turned Anglican minister? Much of its enduring appeal, as I have come to see, is because it speaks to so many universal human experiences that transcend any particular beliefs or doctrines.

Who has not had a time of feeling lost or out of sync with oneself and one's world and then had things pull back together? "I once was lost, but now I'm found." It is a universal human experience to be oblivious or blinded to certain aspects of ourselves or our world and then become awakened to them. "T'was blind but now I see." Who hasn't had a fearful heart at times and then, often through the love and care of others, had that fear relieved? And many of us, I would guess, have had life-changing experiences that have come upon us and have caused us to act, think, see, perceive, and believe in new and different ways for having had them. "How precious did that grace appear the hour I first believed," or the time when I newly perceived, or the time when I saw something in a new and different light for the first time? That's grace at work.

What does it mean then to live by grace? There are several possibilities in addition to the ones already suggested. Living by grace means keeping a stance of openness and receptivity to the unexpected and the sometimes underserved gifts that life can bestow upon us. Shortly after I graduated seminary, I came across a wonderful book by the late Michael Novak titled *Ascent of the Mountain, Flight of the Dove.* Mr. Novak was part of a cadre of radical theologians of the late 1960s who largely wrote against the backdrop of those turbulent times. He later shifted to the ranks of the neoconservatives, which takes nothing away from the timelessness of this book. It is now long out of print. A tattered copy remains on my shelf.

Give heed to the title again: *Ascent of the Mountain, Flight of the Dove.* It's Novak's metaphor for the religious or spiritual journey. Sometimes the life journey, the journey of the spirit, is like climbing a mountain. You work at it, probing, asking questions, seeking answers, despairing at times and hoping at others, being enlightened at times and being completely baffled at other times.

But you keep climbing the mountain, working your way from one level or from one standpoint to the next. Sometimes you may have to backtrack when you're hurt or wounded before you can go any higher. And then in the midst of all that climbing—often when it's least expected—comes the flight of the dove: the moment of sudden inspiration, the sudden sense of the gift-fullness of life. These are the times when we look up from the climb and out across the terrain and say, "Yes, it is good to be here." It is in such moments of grace that we find our reasons and our strengths to continue on with our ascent of the mountain in the faith and in the hope that by grace, we will again, at some point, be blessed by the flight of the dove.

In a dynamic similar to this mountain-dove one, living by grace calls on us to live in the zone between maintaining a trustful attitude toward life and knowing that life will betray us at times. In that chapter on faith, I noted that living by faith means cultivating such an attitude of trust. I used Sam Keen's story about Sylvester the Cat running across a pond to escape the bulldog and how lily pads kept coming up to meet Sylvester's feet so he could keep moving safely along until he starts to worry about where the next lily pad would come from. Keen called this stance *trustful agnosticism*—that is to say, a willingness to trust in life and in your ability to meaningfully walk through life, even if you do not ultimately know just who or what it is you are trusting or where the lily pads are ultimately coming from.

I believe what Sam Keen says. And I also believe what a gentleman named James Hillman says in a book of essays he wrote on trust and betrayal called *A Blue Fire*. He offers a counterpoint to Keen, a yin to the yang. Hillman says,

> You cannot have trust without the possibility of betrayal. . . . We are betrayed only where we truly trust—by brothers, sisters, lovers, spouses, not by enemies (or by someone you don't trust to begin with). Trust has in it the seed of betrayal. Trust and the possibility of betrayal come into the world at the same time. . . . For we must be clear that to live or love only where there is trust, where one cannot be hurt or let down . . . means really being of harm's way, and so to be out of real life.

It took me awhile to get that; and I found myself, upon first reading, arguing with Mr. Hillman. What's wrong with always wanting to be out of harm's way? What's wrong with living and loving only where there is trust? The answer I finally had to give myself was, well, there's nothing really wrong with any of it; it's just that life doesn't always work that way. To choose to let go and trust, as Hillman quite correctly points out, is to also accept the possibility of betrayal. To live by grace, then, is to walk through life with a stance of trust while knowing that the walk is not risk-free but still believing that, by grace, the journey is worth the taking.

I never met or knew Jane Kenyon. I only know her through what little, I must admit, I've read of her work. But I have to believe that, at times and on some level, she had to have felt an ultimate kind of betrayal in knowing that her life would be taken from her before she even reached the age of fifty. And yet she could still celebrate her moments of grace—of eating cercal with sweet milk and peaches and walking with her dog through a New Hampshire wood.

> I got out of bed
> on two strong legs.
> It might have been
> otherwise. I ate
> cereal, sweet
> milk, ripe, flawless
> peach. It might
> have been otherwise.
> I took the dog uphill
> to the birch wood.
> All morning I did
>
> the work I love.
> At noon I lay down
> with my mate. It might
> have been otherwise.
> We ate dinner together
> at a table with silver
> candlesticks. It might
> have been otherwise.
> I slept in a bed
> in a room with paintings
> on the walls, and
> planned for another day
> just like this day.
> But one day, I know,
> it will be otherwise.

Religion is our human response to the dual reality of being alive and knowing we will die. We live by grace, knowing that "one day . . . it will be otherwise."

EPILOGUE

In my first-semester college freshman English class, one of the novels we were assigned was Albert Camus's *The Stranger.*

I found it to be the weirdest book I'd ever read in all my eighteen years. It was something about this French guy named Meursault living in Algeria, whose mother dies and he's not all that affected by her passing. Then he more or less stumbles into committing a murder for which he ends up being sentenced to death. At his trial, the prosecutor makes more of Meursault's seeming indifference to his mother's dying than to his practically inadvertent killing of an Arab, but Meursault gets the guillotine anyway. By the time I finally got to the last page, I was in such a hurry to just be done with the book that I read right past its key passage.

In that passage, Meursault is in his jail cell, a few hours away from his execution. He has just had an angry argument with the prison chaplain who unsuccessfully tried to get him to turn to God while he still had the time. Meursault then notes, "It was as if that great rush of anger [at the chaplain] had washed me clean, emptied me of hope, and, *gazing up at the sky spangled with its signs and stars, for the first time, the first, I laid my heart open to the benign indifference of the universe* [emphasis added]."

As I said, I had no idea what I was reading when I first read those words. Yes, I could easily follow the story line, bizarre as it was, but I couldn't see the point the author was attempting to make. My mind and my thinking at the time were simply not equipped to even catch of glimmer of understanding about what was being said this short novel. A few more years had to go by before I was ready for any kind of engagement with this atheistic existentialist French philosopher, novelist and playwright, Mr. Albert Camus.

As I have moved across the various landscapes of my spirit, the words of Camus's Meursault hover over me and haunt me. I, too, often gaze at a sky "spangled with its signs and stars." And while I am not in a jail cell, awaiting thc guillotine, I view those signs and stars with an awareness—sometimes conscious, sometimes not—of my mortality. What Camus is saying, as I eventually figured out, is that for all our searches for meaning and for all the many life-fulfilling and life-sustaining meanings (with a small *m*) we may derive over the course of our lives, we ultimately live in a universe that is as absurd as the situation in which Meursault found himself. It is also a universe that regards us with what Camus, through the words of his main character in *The Stranger*, calls "benign indifference."

On first take, the phrase "benign indifference" sounds like an oxymoron. Most dictionary definitions of *benign* use words such as "gracious" or "kind" or "favorable." How can a universe regard us in gracious or kind or favorable ways and still be called indifferent? But there is another definition of *benign* that gets closer to what Camus is saying—*not malignant*. We live in a universe, according to Camus, that wishes us no harm (not malignant) and one that is simply indifferent to our existence.

Maybe so, maybe so. I do not discount the possibility. Maybe I live and move and have my being as a creature in a universe that is completely indifferent to my existence. But even if that might be the case, I do not choose to live in a stance of indifference myself. Even if the universe is ultimately indifferent to my existence, I do not have to live as one of its creatures by being indifferent toward it. I find too much joy and pleasure and fulfillment, along with my times of pain and despair and emptiness, as I live my life in one miniscule piece of this vast universe I inhabit that I cannot be indifferent.

So I live in the push and the pull between Updike's Harry Angstrom: "Somewhere behind all this there is something that wants me to find it" and Camus's Meursault "I laid my heart open to the benign indifference of the universe." Which way I lean sometimes depends upon what kind of a day I'm having!

In addition to Updike, my counterpoint to Camus comes from yet another of my Unitarian Universalist ministerial colleagues. This one is the late Reverend Deane Starr. Several years prior to his own passing,

Deane lost a son, Paul, to AIDS in the early 1990s. At a gathering of his fellow clergy members, a few years after Paul had died, Deane related a story of how he came to find some reconciliation with the loss of his son.

He told of how he took a boat cruise off the west coast of Naples, Florida, in the Gulf of Mexico as he continued to deeply grieve his loss about a year after his son's death. Here's how Reverend Starr described the experience:

> The entire sky, from horizon to horizon, was aglow with colors—reds, purples, pinks, and golds. Then the colors faded and the indescribable deep, deep indigo of late twilight filled the sky. Then the boat turned around, and on the eastern horizon was a full and glorious moon.
>
> With tears streaming down my face, I realized that although my son's being had been scattered, he remained a part of this awesome beauty. We can never contain the beauty in which we live and move and have our being. Whether we live or whether we die, we are contained within this beauty.

Deane is saying here that there is an uncontained beauty, a greater web of life, a larger chain of being—some even call it the presence of God—that holds us in our time-bound lives during our time on earth and that also holds the continuing presence of our lives beyond our physical existence. Catching a glimpse of this greater beauty did not remove the reality of the death of Reverend Starr's son. But the experience he described reminded him, as it can remind us, that Life—with a capital *L*—is greater than any one of us, greater than our individual lives.

For me, this is what it all finally comes down to—is it Camus's indifferent universe, or are we "contained within a beauty . . . whether we live or whether we die"?

I ponder on these things, and for all my pondering, I end up back with Iris DeMent:

"I think I'll just let the Mystery be."